The Ethical Practice of Critical Thinking

The Ethical Practice of Critical Thinking

Martin Clay Fowler

DEPARTMENT OF PHILOSOPHY
ELON UNIVERSITY

CAROLINA ACADEMIC PRESS

Durham, North Carolina

Library of Congress Cataloging-in-Publication Data

Fowler, Martin, 1951-
The ethical practice of critical thinking / by Martin Fowler.
p. cm.
Includes bibliographical references and index.
ISBN 10: 1-59460-503-3
ISBN 13: 978-1-59460-503-1 (alk. paper)
1. Critical thinking. 2. Reasoning. 3. Ethics. I. Title.

BC177.F68 2008
160--dc22

2008011854

CAROLINA ACADEMIC PRESS
700 Kent Street
Durham, North Carolina 27701
Telephone (919) 489-7486
Fax (919) 493-5668
www.cap-press.com

Printed in the United States of America

Dedicated to Clyde

Contents

Acknowledgments

I needed a text to address the ethical issues which arise in the social practice of critical thinking skills, so, with the support and arguments of my colleagues in the Philosophy Department of Elon University, I wrote this book. I hope it is the beginning of an extended conversation and discourse about how worthwhile thinking introduces us to worthwhile values and relationships.

For peerless peer review, I extend my gratitude to my colleagues, John Sullivan, Ann Cahill, Nim Batchelor, Anthony Weston, Yoram Lubling, Stephen Schulman, David Johnston, and Joe Cole. They included me in their community discourse and some of them bravely tried out this book in their Critical Thinking classes. Special thanks also to all their students who pondered, argued, objected, and deliberated about the ethics packed within critical thinking. It was a great teacher-student shake-down cruise for this book, the first of many to come. If this book is the last place you expected to be, I hope you're not disappointed. Drop me a note at fowlerm@elon.edu if you have a tough question, helpful suggestion, strenuous objection, or an idea to share. Of course, I will give you full credit if I use your idea in future editions.

Clyde Zuber and I diligently proofed the text and would be grateful for your courtesy in reporting to us any clerical or factual errors. My niece, Andrea Milligan, provided the photos of herself, their family dog, Augustus, and her father, Dr. Richard Milligan. Special thanks to Robert Conrow at Carolina Academic Press for working patiently with me in the preparation of this text.

There's a "Notes and Sources" section at the back of this book to provide students with an extensive annotated bibliography about the books I mention and recommend. A "Notes for Teachers" teaching guide should be available with this text for instructors.

Introduction

Uncovering the Ethics in Critical Thinking

Ethics is the last place I expected to be when I began teaching philosophy because I taught both "critical thinking" and "ethical practice" as separate courses. I hadn't yet thought much about critical thinking as an ethical practice in its own right. We casually treat thought and behavior as two independent kingdoms, so we don't hunt commonalities. For example, in critical thinking, you could distinguish form (critical thinking) from its content (such as ethics), or you might draw a distinction between the structure of argument (logic) and its techniques (rhetoric). Our distinctions quickly harden into pairs of mutually exclusive terms with no place for the human relationships created in the activity of critical thinking. A pair of distinctions which takes itself too seriously will try to carve up the world between them. A long argument with others can have unexpected detours, breakthroughs, reversals, and, after patience and luck, insights that stun and transform us. Our distinctions might miss all that. So, as the roses on the rhetoric and deduction wilt, don't forget how hard it was to work out understanding of issues and topics, despite great differences in perspective, lack of information, stubborn conflicts, and so much being at stake. We shouldn't forget the ethics inside critical thinking.

Discovering that ethics not only makes critical thinking come alive also allows us to give due recognition and honor to an under-celebrated part of our ethical life: *making arguments which matter, about things which matter, with people who matter to each other.* Ethics is about showing respect, extending charity, achieving the best outcome, and keeping each other honest, which are values we actively sustain when we persist in our best thinking together.

When you are taught critical thinking, you learn to identify an argument's conclusion and the credibility of its premises. You may be introduced to new terms such as "valid" or "sound" arguments, and you're cautioned to spot and avoid invalid or fallacious inferences. You discover that critical thinking involves not only logic, but understanding causal correlations, reasoning by analogy, or applying standards to assess available evidence in support of a position.

Even creative problem-solving is part of critical thinking. Learn this, and you should be the very model of a critical thinker ready to set sail, eyes fixed on the horizon, hands firmly on the helm, captain of your ship of intellect, like the photo of Yours Truly.

Actually, it's not my yacht. In fact, I don't know how to sail. The real owner and pilot is busy outside the frame of the picture, adjusting the rigging to take advantage of the breeze on Puget Sound. He trusted me for a few minutes to pay attention to the wind, keep the yacht moving in a more or less straight line, and avoid ramming any other boats (also outside the frame of the picture). It's not a bad metaphor for ethical argumentation. Real sailing, like real arguing, involves coordination and adjustment between people and with the elements at hand. It can be tricky to work with others to keep an argument on track without veering off course or winding up in a collision. It requires trust. It only looks as though you could manage it alone and single-handedly.

That brings us to the puppy. This is a very hungry little dog since no one has reached out to feed this unnamed pitiful puppy. Why bother? After all, it's featured in this book only as a teaching tool to make a point about critical thinking. Yes, it's a *starving* teaching tool, and we feel bad or should feel bad about not feeding the dog, but thinking is not about feelings, right? Why should an animal's appetite or our guilt matter to logic? Why should what we do or not do about the precious puppy matter if we're just learning how to think clearly about this canine? We either reason cogently about this neglected heart-breaking pup which depends entirely upon us for its very life, or we don't.

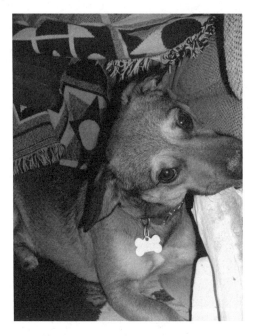

So, at the risk of committing a string of fallacies such as begging the question (How long have you been starving this puppy?) and appeals to emotion (the right conclusion is the one which feels good to us), we must concede that it's hard to keep thinking about the puppy without considering what matters to us, what we ought to do, and how we can think of a way to help the puppy. That yearning and questioning is not necessarily a distraction from reasoning. We've uncovered ethics hiding inside critical thinking.

Critical thinking, like any sustained, complex human activity which affects people, does have a rich ethical landscape. That landscape concerns what we can call "sustaining arguments." A sustaining argument keeps a discussion alive and growing by upholding worthy standards of critical thinking. A sustaining argument supports the members of the community by unfolding so as to respect their dignity and their need to think together and make decisions about things which matter for them. Finally, the sustaining argument protects and honors community of discourse itself as a place which is worth arguing in. In fact, to use sustaining arguments to think critically well, at length, and about topics that matter calls for certain principles. Sustaining arguments show certain principles:

1. Sustaining arguments respect the intelligence and humanity of the both the arguer and intended audience by helping rather than hindering our ability to think, and by supporting rather than undermining a community of discourse. We can achieve this by applying the **principle of charitable interpretation**: choose the most plausible interpretation of the arguer's words and the best reasoning to be found in those words. A necessary skill for practicing this principle is **objectivity**.

2. Sustaining arguments prove something worth discussing, allow questioning which decisions are worth considering, or lead to commitments worth making. We can achieve this by applying the **principle of substance**: choose only matters and issues for arguments which deserve your best thinking, facilitate necessary decisions, and in which there are stakes that matter for the benefit or detriment of all concerned. A necessary skill for practicing this principle is **suffering**. Feeling pain takes no skill, of course, but learning how to best bear one's pain or share the pain of others does demand learning and proficiency. Also, if you haven't suffered

or at least known pain, you probably haven't thought much or very well about what really matters.

3. Sustaining arguments are also necessarily good arguments which are factually based and logically coherent. We can achieve this by applying the **principle of scholarship**: Acknowledge and deal with the obstacles to knowledge effectively enough to investigate the truth of propositions, test the strength of inferences, and evaluate the merits of an argument. A necessary skill for practicing this principle is **curiosity**. Scholarship which is not inquisitive has not applied this principle adequately. Scholarship may involve accurately cited quotes and footnotes, but making references without digging for knowledge and understanding doesn't apply the principle of scholarship adequately. Scholarship is not only courteous but nosey too.

4. Sustaining arguments are also arguments which strengthen a community as it confronts and learns from the conflicts, impasses, failures, and sacrifices which are part of arguing together as a community. We can achieve this by applying the **principle of conflict.** Acknowledge that any good argument invites conflict[1] and that the community of discourse is charged with working effectively through the conflicts in its arguments. The community is sustained by the way that it handles its conflicts in argument. A necessary skill to apply this principle is that of **sufficiency.** That's the skill of knowing when "enough is enough" and a conflict cannot usefully move further without major changes.

---

1. A short and excellent book on this subject is *The Little Book of Conflict Transformation* by John Paul Lederach (Good Books, 1969). Lederach provides a map and framework for navigating conflict in ways that ultimately transform rather than destroy relationships. According to Lederach, argument does not resolve conflict in a steady path of progress. It may progress, then stall, regress or even fall apart only to transform in better ways. The path is more spiral than linear. Each stage is a "sufficiency" rather than as a terminus. Perhaps if we don't impose this ages and stages approach *a priori* but instead use and test it empirically, we can better navigate and even transform seemingly irreconcilable conflicts.

By way of further introduction, the ethics we find inside critical thinking leads us not only into arguments, but also into fallacies, reasoning about numbers, and reconciling conflicts. Happily, we wind up with the community of people willing to think together. This club, gang, committee, society, pack, salon, or team may be a predictable pod of kindred spirits, or a surprise kaleidoscopic community of like-minded souls. When we started thinking, it's the last place we expected to be, but it won't be such a bad destination.

It's hard to think of a subject for critical thinking that you could pursue entirely on your own or which is so completely removed from human concerns and consequences that it could have no ethical implications whatsoever. My undergraduate choice would have been figuring out how to conjugate and remember German verbs in an 8:00 a.m. class. I really had no plans to ever visit Germany. Still, learning German meant learning how to communicate and taking responsibility for how I would use this skill. I consoled myself that the mental exercise was valuable all by itself. At the very least, I encouraged my instructor who complimented me on showing up and having the nerve to form complete sentences even when I lacked the correct vocabulary. (At least I think it was a compliment.) Thirty years later, I encountered some German tourists in Thailand who turned to me for help. You just never know what ethical opportunities might be opened by your critical thinking skills.

So, why argue instead of just sitting down to talk about what matters to you, in German or otherwise? Why does critical thinking depend on arguments? A conversation which makes a good argument does more than share thoughts. You help each other to link thoughts together in a trustworthy way. The conversation uncovers the destination of those linked thoughts and the fact that they actually *do* have a destination. Yes, we also need to express ourselves. And we need to reflect, remember, plan, and get perspective. Conversation helps meet all those needs. But conversing through an argument allows us to remain objective enough for honest thinking and curious enough to persist in our scholarship together. It leads us to learn from each other's suffering as to what's worth arguing about, and to know when we've argued enough. "Critical" thinking is not just analysis. It's the skilled exercise of our full range of cognitive skills together. That's why it's also an ethical practice.

Let me say a few words about the "**shares**." In other texts, these items are called "exercises," "assignments" or "homework." Those terms imply that the author gives you instructions about how to perform a pre-conceived task. The author and perhaps a teacher expect you to learn something worthwhile from accomplishing the task. By doing the exercise, task, or assignment, you may get a reward such as a good grade. Expectations and rewards make up one sort of ethical relationship between the author of the textbook and the student who reads it. You're expected do the work and get a reward for your labor. It's appropriate to teaching skills, figuring out problems, or memorizing information. If that assignment isn't part of your homework, you skip it.

However, the *ethical practice* of critical thinking, calls for a different relationship. You and I belong to a community of discourse. We're dealing with issues that don't simply matter to me or to you alone. You have a bigger stake than a one-time grade or storing up some learning. Therefore, you have a *share* in this community. It's not very likely that you'll have to do all fifty of these shares as homework, but don't skip any of them. Each share teaches about the ethical practice of critical thinking, so be patient and read through them. I'm sharing something with you. You're hereby allowed, empowered, entitled and otherwise invited to enjoy them even when they aren't building your grade or your work ethic.

Do you remember being told to share when you were a child? That's one of the first ethical practice lessons we receive as children. Think of sharing both ways. If you are in a classroom, share what you learn with others, not just with the teacher. You are a shareholder in this community, but being a shareholder also means sharing what you learn with other shareholders. That's not a bad first definition of scholarship.

For example, we shut our underfed puppy inside a container to think about him critically and without distractions. He's confined for the sake of argument. We now think hard about the whimpering puppy, as such, but we share no food with him. What do you suppose he'll share when he finally gets out of that box? Critical thinking is also a real relationship with others, so be nice and share your shares..

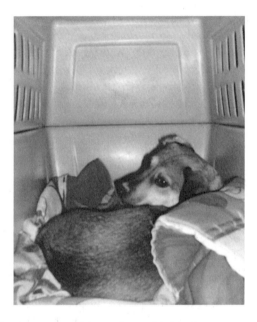

The fifty shares spread throughout this book are your portfolio in the ethics of critical thinking. You may share your shares with your teacher alone, but you're also working with others and learning from them. Each share is more than a fleeting relationship between your eyes and a book. Each scholar quoted in this book shares something with you. Think of it as a gift, if you like. If you really can't use a particular gift, pass it along to someone who'll enjoy the gift and your generosity. If you don't like it at all, keep in mind that these are gifts for which it really is the thought that counts. Keep thinking.

Your first three shares are about maps. Did you ever think of drawing a map as critical thinking? A map requires clear, consistent relationships among accurately represented items. The map should be complex enough to be complete, but not so complex that it becomes cluttered. If the map marks directions, it's analogous to making a good argument which leads to a conclusion. But maps, like arguments, are also ethical enterprises. We're expected to trust and rely upon them. To draw a map, we pick sites which matter to a particular community, point out boundaries and causeways, show where we and others belong and keep people from getting lost. When we follow a map, we participate in those relationships. Centuries ago, explorers' maps could be state secrets. Stealing or falsifying a map could have serious consequences. As a type of thinking together, mapmaking and map-following are ethical practices.

Share No. 1 How do you make a map for something which has no context? Perhaps nothing simply crawls out from under a rock, drops from outer space, or pops into being through spontaneous generation, but sometimes an item confronts us very much like that. It's a challenge to think critically about something which has no apparent connection to any of our familiar points of reference. Let's start with a *tamper*. Are you a tamper? Do you have a tamper? Are tampers good or bad? If you're uncertain, work with the verb. You know that "tampering" can mean interfering in a harmful way. But consider that you can tamp too much into your glove compartment or trash compactor. So, tamping is cramming or mashing some aggregate into a small space. A vegetable juicer uses a plastic tamper to compress pulp. Thinking about this has no ethical shadows, colors, or mass yet. But consider that you only tamp something which you're willing to treat roughly, almost as refuse. You don't mash, crush, or tamp compassionately or with much respect for what you cram. (Think about that when you cram for a final exam …)

Now pick a different sort of "tamper" such as 55 Cancri. This is 41 light years from earth, yet, as you think critically about its physical relationships, questions of human value and meaning also arise. Unexpectedly, thinking about 55 Cancri shapes our own ethical practice. Look up this "tamper" or another news, science, or business topic that has currently has no context for you. Next, brainstorm about how this topic affects people's lives. Keep thinking until you discover how thinking about it with others affects how people treat each other and their world. You aren't making unlikely connections between unrelated things. As a critical thinker, you're putting a new topic on the "ethics map" of human values, concerns, relationships, needs, and aspirations. You're building a context nest for your new topic. The connections already exist. You're uncovering and articulating them. What kind of ethical issues (rights, duties, values, virtues, benefit, harm, principles, good vs. evil, right vs. wrong) come up? Try to find either a subject so specialized that your group ("community of discourse") has no expertise about it, or take a very mundane area of research (e.g. fertilizers or food packaging) and show an ethical issue that your group might otherwise have never considered. Show why this "tamper" matters for us. Write a 5-page research paper on this new topic.

> "It is notorious that (Francis) Bacon regularly described scientific activity in oddly savage imagery, incorporating violent conquest as a central part of his original myth of scientific supremacy. Bacon repeatedly insisted that the aim of the new science must not be just to 'exert a gentle guidance over Nature's course' but 'to conquer and subdue her, to shake her to her foundation.'"
> — *Science and Poetry* by Mary Midgley (2001)

Great thinkers are more often posthumously blamed than praised for all consequences of their ideas and arguments. If future generations really could file class action suits for reparations from past philosophers, I suspect there would be much less philosophizing or at least much less interesting philosophy. Questions of blame and praise aside, ideas and arguments help or hinder people in their thinking and can be expected to take on a life of their own beyond our needs and understanding and beyond their original community of discourse. Prof. Mary Midgley argues that the 16th century philosopher, Francis Bacon argued so persuasively that science is a conquest of nature, that this way of thinking eventually became sufficiently ingrained in Western culture such that our environment has been conquered to the point of devastation and rapid extinction of thousands of species. If she's right, that's quite a serious legacy. Words can inflict massive historical damage.

Influential thinking has moral consequences, but that doesn't mean that we simply moralize with hindsight about unforeseen ethical ramifications of past thinking. For example, a great deal of thinking has gone into extraction, refining, production, marketing, transportation, and utilization of petroleum over the past century. This thinking led to increased carbon emissions, pollution, global warming, and environmental crisis. We shouldn't fault past thinkers for what they could not predict. We might fault them (and ourselves) for thinking as if problem-solving were self-contained and autonomous in a way which dispenses with ethical burdens. We can do that when we shrug and say "It's just a job." Doing critical thinking, whether for pay or not, as though it could have nothing to do with ethical practice is culpable because it means thinking together as though treating others and our shared world with respect, compassion, and care is justifiably irrelevant.

Share No. 2 I invite you to do Internet and library research about Project Chariot. When you discover what this project was about forty years ago, it will be very tempting to retrospectively moralize about its ethics. Resist the temptation. Write a 5-page research paper about the kinds of critical thinking which the project required: scientific, political, economic, and military. Identify any ethical issues which this thinking uncovered, created, or tried to bury. Which features of this ethical practice were unknown to the critical thinkers on all sides involved in Project Chariot? Which features were considered unimportant? Think of this as an ethical map of the sort of public thinking carried out in this project.

Share No. 3 For your third share, you get to map yourself. A widely shared and feared human experience is being lost. One of the promises which a map implies is protection against being or staying lost. "You are here." If you're on a college campus, look at the buildings around you, draw a map of the campus which would be accurate enough to guide an incoming first year student to classes at your college. Then check to see how accurate it really is. Next, draw a map of the social geography of your college. A first-year student can't locate himself or herself unless they know what groups they belong in or don't belong in. What features would the map contain and where would you find yourself? Would the first-year student be in the middle, on the bottom, the center, on the margins, or elsewhere? What sort of ethical questions would an incoming first year student ask upon examining your social map of your college? (Does the map imply that some people are not good enough to belong in some groups?) The map below is for my campus, Elon University. Write an essay containing your map and your proposed ethical questions. If you're not in college, draw a map of your place of employment (Good luck if you do your work online!) to orient a new employee, and then draw a map of the social geography. It's not necessarily the same as a chart of the personnel dept.'s management structure. It may not be a treasure map, but it's still a gift to help folks find themselves and what's expected of them. Don't simply turn this map in as an "assignment." *Share it and explain it to three other people first.*

"Invention of the weather map around 1816 raises perhaps the most intriguing question in the history of environmental cartography: What took them so long? ... lacking exemplars to mimic and spatial hypotheses to test, no one thought that cartographic snapshots of barometric pressure and wind might prove revealing ... Heinrich Wilhelm Brandes argued that plotting graphic symbols on a map would be more revealing than merely listing the data." —*Air Apparent—How Meteorology Learned to Map, Predict, and Dramatize the Weather* by Mark Monmonier (1999)

Mark Monmonier suggests that the lack of weather maps before 1816 was not due to the absence of modern technology but rather an inability to think of weather as mapable. People thought that only stable landmarks such as oceans and continents were suitable for maps. Because we see dynamic computer-generated weather maps on TV each day, it is hard to conceive that the very project of mapping the weather was once inconceivable. Perhaps the Internet will be mapable one day. That would be a useful though risky map.

Share No. 4 Write a 3-page essay about how a reliable and widely available Internet map would make an ethical difference for your decisions. Illustrate your essay by drawing a map of the Internet. Decide the purpose of your map. Would you want to restrict access to your map? Would your map show servers, search engines, domains, users, sites, or other items? If you're "on the Internet," then where, if anywhere, are you on the map? Research online for topographical models of the Internet. Some models map domain densities or other features of the Internet. A traffic map and a geological map can both be good maps of the same area. Would your map keep people from getting lost in the "area" of cyberspace?

You are here. What are you going to do about it?

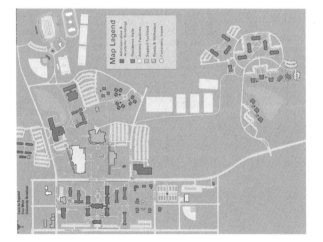

The Ethical Practice of
Critical Thinking

Chapter One

Sustaining Arguments

What is a Sustaining Argument? When I worked in a law firm, attorneys would refer to a monetary judgment awarded by the court for a creditor against a penniless debtor as a judgment "suitable for framing"—meaning that the creditor could take satisfaction from receiving justice but couldn't expect to take anything from the debtor. Even if the creditor gets the debtor evicted, the judgment isn't going to result in money for the creditor if the debtor has no assets. It's unenforceable. This is somewhat analogous to making an argument which is factually based and logically reasoned to the point that the conclusion is virtually inescapable, only to find that your audience refuses to accept the conclusion or acknowledge the merit of your argument. You are left with an argument "suitable for framing." Sometimes this happens because the topic is controversial for your audience. Your experience with discussions about environmental crises, abortion, or same-sex marriage might have taught you that, if your audience does not *wish or want* a conclusion to be true, then there is a very good chance that the conclusion will never be reached, no matter how compelling the evidence or the logic.

So why can't a valid and sound argument carry the day all by itself? Shouldn't logic and sound reasoning be self-sufficient, invincible, compelling, and redeeming values that will irresistibly commend your argument to any and all honest thinkers of good faith? The fact that such arguments fall upon deaf ears means that we need to consider social and ethical issues too. Rather than thinking of yourself as a voice crying in the wilderness or blaming your audience for being close-minded and intellectually dishonest, think about this impasse as a social challenge for you as a critical thinker. A good argument with no fans has somehow failed to commend itself as a way to help people to think or has ignored or failed to create, sustain, or help to constitute the relationships that sustained thinking requires. What could you do to overcome this difficulty?

Actually, there are two difficulties. The first is the exasperation of finding no audience for a good argument. The second is the affront of subjecting an audience to an argument which is a complete waste of their time. An argument which people can't or won't engage isn't likely to sustain them or their community. An argument which doesn't deal with the audience's true needs and interests can't matter for them. So, once you have an argument that is valid and sound (in deductive terms) or which is as trustworthy as you can make it in terms of available evidence and the implications of that evidence, in inductive terms, consider holding your argument to the ethical standard of a **sustaining argument**.[1]

A "sustaining argument" supports people, their community, and the very practice of critical thinking.

A "sustaining argument" (a) *sustains* the discussion itself by up-

---

1. "Sustainable" is the best word I know to describe arguments in their ethical practice. I concede that "sustainable" can be not-so-innocently packed with ambiguity and hidden assumptions. There's the hidden assumption that being sustainable is necessarily a good thing, regardless of what's being sustained. As an example of ambiguity, we try to make a business environmentally "sustainable" in three ways at once: (a) keep the current business and the ecosystem status quo perpetual, (b) preserve the business, nature, or both, as a bequest for future generations, and (c) gratify present customer or stockholder needs without trashing nature. These goals might be compatible, but they're different. A "sustaining" argument isn't a never-ending discourse foisted upon future generations. It sustains in a number of interdependent and important ways. Standards of critical thinking, respect for persons and their needs, collaborative scholarship, and resilient communities of discourse are necessary for optimal critical thinking. Sustaining them is what critical thinking *ought* to do. We just need to remain clear about how any given argument sustains.

holding worthy standards of critical thinking, (b) *sustains* the members of the community by arguing so as to respect their dignity and their need to think together and make decisions about things which matter for them, and (c) *sustains* the community of discourse itself as a place which is worth arguing in. Why all three? If we're looking for a normative ethical standard for arguments to endorse, we recognize that we need to tend not just to the activity (arguing) but also to the community and its members that make arguing possible. In a community of discourse, we're responsible for more than making a point. We're responsible for making the point as well as possible. We're further responsible for how we treat each other when we make the point. And we try to make our community a place worthy of our best thinking and best relationships.

Sustaining arguments are arguments which matter, about things which matter, to people who matter to each other. While there's no guarantee that a sustaining argument will open all deaf ears or always find a community's real needs, it's a standard which makes hearing and finding more likely. Here are some features of a sustaining argument:

A. Arguments Which Respect Intelligence and Humanity

Sustaining arguments respect the intelligence and humanity of the both the arguer and intended audience by helping rather than hindering our ability to think, and by supporting rather than undermining a community of discourse. Not all arguers are blessed with intelligence or complete information, and even the brightest debaters can commit fallacies. However, we can do our best with the information and tools available such that an argument can manifest the very best thinking of which we're capable. Then we can ask: *Does the argument allow people to better understand what they are arguing about? Are they better able to continue thinking about the subject with each other as a result of the argument?* If not, then the argument and the discussion fail to be sustaining, even if it is logically valid and its conclusion is well-supported.

For example, I work with a church group that visits jail inmates on Saturday mornings. This particular jail is hardly an optimal think tank. It's more of a brood, worry, rage, grieve, and wait tank. The inmates in this facility are mainly men who are awaiting trial and are too poor to afford bail. They're separated from their jobs and families for days, weeks, or months at a time. When I meet one of these inmates, I don't know whether he's clever or stupid. I don't know what he has been charged with, or whether he's guilty. They're all wearing orange jumpsuits. I do introduce myself, ask the person's name and then ask, "How can I help?"

Whether it's talking about family, planning for the future, picking a greeting card, or praying together, we find ways to respect each other's intelligence and humanity. Though we're separated from inmates by Plexiglas, this brief give and take relationship is a form of respect that this person typically doesn't receive from others while incarcerated. How you talk is at least as important as *what* you talk about. In a warehouse for humans, you can still forge a community.

When you respect someone's intelligence, that doesn't mean you necessarily regard that person as an authority, that you automatically defer to their judgment at the expense of your own, or even that you have a particularly favorable impression of their I.Q. It does mean that you give people the attention and your best efforts to assist their thinking, because that is what you would want in return. You respect humanity in the ways you speak with others or write for others. You show that you understand that you are not watching T.V. or putting data into a computer. Respect is not just an attitude. It's also learning the rhythm and risk of allowing each other to have a point of view and to be taken seriously.

B. Arguments Which Matter

Sustaining arguments prove something worth discussing, allow decisions worth considering, or lead to commitments worth making. A sustaining argument is never something offered solely "for the sake of argument." You still might argue hypothetically or playfully, but, if the argument is to really sustain a community's members, you can't start arguing from a standpoint of complete detachment, alienation, or self-absorption, and proceed to argue with indifference to the perspective and background of the audience and the welfare of the community of discourse to which you and your audience belong. A sustaining argument may even be about something exotic, esoteric, technical, or abstract, but its good reasons will also be good for the community's discourse.

Sadly, some people give good reasons a very bad name. I'm thinking of Pat (not his or her real name). You may know a Pat. Whenever Pat is caught in a mistake, lie, or other misdeed that hurts the community of discourse, Pat invariably comes up with "good reasons." In fact, Pat has turned manufacturing excuses into a veritable one-person cottage industry, busily producing arguments and justifications which serve no purpose other than to get Pat off the hook or to blame someone else. Pat is also fond of using the group as an audience for airing personal gripes regardless of the group's discussion topic. You can be sure that Pat will contrive to steer any discussion of issues to Pat's own concerns. And Pat always has good reasons for doing so. Good reasons that do not help the community to think through issues and work towards decisions that are necessary and important for the group just aren't good for very much. So much for "Pat" answers.

> "In ecology and evolution, diversity in gender and sexuality is denigrated by sexual selection theory, a perspective that can be traced to Darwin. This theory preaches that males and females obey certain univer-

sal templates — the passionate male and the coy female — and that deviations from these templates are anomalies. Yet the facts of nature falsify Darwin's sexual selection theory ... Scientists are professionally responsible for refuting claims that homosexuality is unnatural. The dereliction of this responsibility has caused homosexual people to suffer persecution as a result of false premises of 'unnaturalness.'" — *Evolution's Rainbow* by Joan Roughgarden (2004)

Here's a test of how far we can extract ethics from critical thinking. Dr. Roughgarden champions proper ethical regard for homosexuals not as a moral duty imposed upon biology, but as a pre-existing and ongoing ethical relationship that exists as biologists do their research. How they stand up for good scholarship, charitable interpretation of the data, upholding substantial matters for concern, and participating in social and religious conflict would be part of biology as a community of discourse. Biologists might disagree with Roughgarden's specific thesis about sexual selection or disagree with her broader thesis about the ethics within biological research, but it's a dramatic test, isn't it?

The idea that homosexuality is "unnatural" goes back to ancient Greek and Roman commentary on human behavior and contextualizing of early Christian epistles. The label places an exception outside the observed generalities of nature with which non-homosexuals identify. It also expresses moral disapproval by implying that it is outside sanctioned behavior. In a cosmic sense, the word "unnatural" is odd, for if nature is everything, no item can be outside to nature. Where in the world would it be?

Share No. 5 Let's take a different example dealing with sustainability and what is natural. Food is the most basic example of what we mean by "sustenance," isn't it? If food doesn't sustain, then it hardly counts as food. Go to your nearest fast-food restaurant and order a meal. As you eat, do good scholarship and describe carefully what you are eating. Make notes on how each item looks, tastes, and smells. Research the calories and nutritional benefits of the food. You may find consumer handouts in the restaurant to get you started. Otherwise, research these facts online.

Now make a list of what is natural and what is unnatural about your meal. You may want to finish eating before you start describing. Chemicals added to food are not "natural" if they weren't part of the original potatoes or meat. But that's tricky. All nature consists of chemicals, right? How about the colors, flavors, and smells? Fast food is usually thawed frozen material that is quite old and shipped from far away. If it doesn't taste, smell, or look that way, so you may need to put your experience in the "unnatural" column. Finally, argue whether this is a substantial issue for people who eat at this restaurant. They're not exactly a community of discourse, but should they be? What do you think? Is the price of the food the only substantial issue for you and for them?

C. Arguments Which Uphold Critical Thinking

If an argument matters in the ways we've discussed, then it matters enough to be *well-argued*. Sustaining arguments are also necessarily good arguments which are factually based and logically coherent. You might be skeptical about this statement. After all, since communities of discourse seem to be greatly influenced by very bad arguments which appear in the media, why can't certain bad arguments be considered "sustaining" too, at least for advertisers and politicians? A bad argument may create profit for someone and a certain solidarity of opinion, but a bad argument also disrespects intelligence, hinders people's ability to think, and often is offered to end discourse rather than to sustain or promote it. Even though bad arguments can confer a pragmatic advantage, they don't have what it takes to be genuinely sustaining arguments. How good does an argument need to be? No argument is perfect, and you can uncover some weakness in any argument's logic or have legitimate doubts about the truth of some of its propositions.

The point is that the argument's genuine strengths, whatever they are, are necessary for the argument to be sustaining, despite whatever weaknesses it may have. "Sustaining" isn't just a neutral label that can apply equally to good and bad arguments. All sustaining arguments are good, but not all good arguments are sustaining. An argument which embodies the best standards of critical thinking available to the community does more than advance the argument. It also lifts up the community.

How good an argument would it take to convince you to face an empty plate, day after day? Because I fast from time to time, I've studied plenty of arguments for and against fasting. Those who try and like fasting argue that it confers wonderful spiritual and physical benefits for anyone and everyone (since it worked for them). Others who won't try it or tried it only to find it difficult and unpleasant, generalize to argue that only a fool would voluntarily do something so senseless and risky as abstaining from food. Neither of these arguments is particularly sustaining. How do you know whether they would apply to you if you stopped eating?

The very best arguments I've heard reflect research on how the body actually handles a fast, acknowledge that people can differ quite a bit in their physiological reactions to fasting, and recognize many spiritual traditions that give meaning and focus to a fast. These "sustaining" arguments reflect a comprehensive and diverse understanding of fasting disciplines, as well as some humility about not having all the answers that work for everyone. Even if you're not eating with your friends, don't go without sustenance until you have a sustaining argument.

Then too, an argument which sustains a discussion isn't one that just keeps it going indefinitely. Although persistence and patience can be very useful virtues when you argue, the goal is not to keep people talking until they drop. Later in this book, we'll call this the ethical skill of "sufficiency" of knowing when enough is enough in an argument, and knowing the ways to then proceed. A discussion is sustained when the participants uphold and observe the best standards of thinking available to them, sustain their respect for each other, and sustain their community of discourse. That may mean agreeing to move on to a new argument at some point.

There are some principles that help to guide us in the direction of sustaining arguments: charity in argument, arguing about matters of substance, applying good scholarship, and how to expect and deal with conflict. These are the topics for the next chapter.

Share No. 6 In critical thinking, it's easier and more fun to detect a fallacious argument than it is to construct a good argument. But making a good argument is work worth doing. Let's start with the fun part. Write a three-page dialogue between two students which is appallingly unsustaining. You've probably overheard or contributed to a conversation on an issue which seemed like a waste of time. If you can't remember one, make up a dialogue on some topic so that the dialogue is *not* a sustaining argument. Perhaps the topic doesn't really matter to the speakers. It's not "substantial" for them. Perhaps that conversation treats others as if they don't matter. Cram it, pack it, (and tamp it) full of fallacies, bad manners, and self-absorbed banter. Sadly, this isn't very difficult, is it?

Next, pick a topic which you really care about and make it the topic of a three-page argument dialogue. In your dialogue, show individuals having a sustaining argument about a topic which really matters to you. This is harder, but it's good practice for the real thing. You don't have to make the dialogue persuasive or perfect, just sustaining. How would the two talk and behave towards each other about the topic you cherish, in ways which honor the four principles of charity, scholarship, substance, and conflict?

I know a student who did a class presentation arguing against the Americans With Disabilities Act of 1990 on the grounds that providing accommodations for the handicapped is an expensive and unjustifiable burden upon employers and public facilities. He marshaled his facts about the costs, the relatively small number of people who directly benefit from handicap access and accommodations, and he concluded that the Act should be repealed since it did not benefit the majority and placed an unfair financial burden upon them. He argued for his position very cogently, though it was a bit one-sided. However, he seemed oblivious to the fact that at least one person in his audience was seated in a wheelchair and another was wearing a hearing aid. How do you suppose they felt while listening to this argument? I'm guessing that the student didn't regard himself as belonging with his audience in a community of discourse. The problem wasn't simply rudeness. He spoke as if the actual needs of his listeners could not make any difference to his argument.

Share No. 7 No one except clowns really try to make fools of themselves when they're sharing their thoughts. Yet it happens too often, especially when the speaker is clueless about the needs or perspective of the listeners. It's a real gift to spare someone this embarrassment. Think of people making arguments about ethics, politics, or religion without much awareness of the real needs, interests, or perspectives of those listening. You can use professors as examples, but don't provide names. Think outside the classroom too. Preachers, advertisers, politicians, campus leaders, job supervisors, or family members make clueless arguments. In a three-page essay, describe the situation and how the argument seemed not simply unpopular but badly suited for its intended audience. Describe how the argument could have been presented in a sustaining way, respecting listeners, respecting standards of good reasoning, and respecting the community to which both the speaker and listeners belong. *Share your share no. 7 with at least two other people.*

Astronomer Timothy Ferris argues for some skepticism or at least caution in drawing conclusions about the existence of intelligent life elsewhere in the universe:

"Two scientists, both using the same facts and both innocent of logical errors, can reach wildly different estimates of the abundance of intelligent life in the universe. Why? Because it's exceedingly difficult to make reliable calculations of probability based on a single example. If you draw the king of hearts from a magician's deck of cards, how are you to calculate the odds of your having drawn that particular card if you don't know the contents of the rest of deck? You can't. You need to see more of the cards." *The Whole Shebang—A State of the Universe(s) Report* by Timothy Ferris (1997)[2]

If Prof. Ferris is right, then we do not have any basis at present for concluding with certainty whether intelligent non-human life exists. Ferris' point seems to be that we don't know enough yet to argue with confidence for or against the existence of non-human intelligent life. So how are we supposed to reason about it? Perhaps the key to getting an argument off the ground is to figure out what sort of evidence would be helpful and what principles might guide our search for evidence.

Share No. 8 As your critical thinking community seeks out non-human critical thinkers, you need to both understand and

---

2. This is not the fallacy of "appeal to ignorance." Ferris doesn't claim that alien intelligence exists because it isn't disproved or that it must *not* exist because no one has yet proven its existence. Ferris claims that intelligence on earth is insufficient evidence to conclusively confirm or deny alien intelligence elsewhere. An excellent guide to thinking about this sort of question is *How to Think About Weird Things: Critical Thinking for a New Age* by Theodore Schick and Lewis Vaughn (McGraw Hill, 2001). Can we assume that intelligence announces itself when we have the right clues? Intelligence can also be subtle, coy, ambiguous or weird. What sort(s) of evidence do we need most? What are the best ways of getting that evidence? What's it really worth to us? Since Ferris' book was published, over two hundred extrasolar planets have been discovered. What questions should our community ask? Is human intelligence really the most reliable (if the only available) template for identifying other kinds of intelligence?

respect intelligence. Intelligence needs to be greeted and invited, not just targeted. So, the quest is an ethical practice. To truly join and belong to your community, the language barrier might not be insurmountable. The real obstacle would be agreeing as to what is worth thinking about. Forget spaceships and gadgets. Think about the challenges of rearing the young, dealing with conflict and danger, achieving social unity, learning games, and finding food. Go outside on a clear night and train your binoculars on the constellation Cancer. March is the best month to see this constellation though anytime between January and June will work. Its stars are dim, but it's right between the constellations Leo and Gemini. Draw a picture of the stars you observe and identify them. Cancer is the location of the star 55 Cancri which has five planets around it. Meditate quietly for ten minutes upon this constellation as you observe it and decide what you would most want to think about with any intelligence living there. Write down your answer in a three-page essay and explain how you would make sharing this critical thinking an ethical practice as well.

"Knowledge is increasing every day and our rate of acquiring knowledge is accelerating." True or false? Most people would agree with this assessment, even though students and the general public do not seem very well informed about basic history, science, or current events when they have to answer questions on these subjects. If knowledge is really increasing, why is this so? Worse than that, we have a great deal of misinformation. Then too, as you study any subject beyond an introductory course, you discover that its scholars and researchers have doubts, disputes, and uncertainties. It's a fallacy of division (assuming that what's true of the whole is necessarily true of its parts) to conclude that because mankind in general is amassing knowledge, that you or your community of discourse automatically receives any sustaining crumb of it. You can still starve on the information highway, no matter how smart humankind becomes.

Share No. 9 Real scholarship requires enough humility to admit when you don't have enough information or understanding to form an opinion on a topic yet. This humility is hardest when you are already set in your opinions on a topic. Get together with four other people and form a temporary discussion club. Take turns presenting your views to each other on same-sex marriage. Listen patiently and attentively without interrupting or attacking anyone in your club. Make notes about the points which were raised. Next, figure out whether your group presented more than one side to the issue. If not, why was only one side offered in your club? Is there a legitimate reason for that, or is something missing from your community of discourse? Perhaps someone was too shy or too intimidated to disagree with the others. Finally, confer with each other and make a list of all the places in the world where same sex couples can legally marry each other. List places in the world where they can have civil unions or register their domestic partners. Then do some on-line research and find out the actual answers to these questions. Better yet, interview some same-sex couples. How well did your club do on its initial presentation on this topic? State the sort of information you think your community of discourse needs to know about same-sex marriage before anyone should take your club's views on the subject seriously.

"In very limited ways, the future of the Nobel Prizes seems predictable. Scientific discoveries of Nobel caliber can be expected to continue as far as one can see; too little is yet understood about too much ... Peace prizes will hardly lack laureates, since war and injustice are permanent as death, though the character of the awards may change as circumstances do ... ." —*The Nobel Prize: A History of Genius, Controversy, and Prestige* by Burton Feldman (2000)

"We are like the explorers of a great continent who have penetrated to its margins in most points of the compass and have mapped the major mountain chains and rivers. There are still innumerable details to fill in, but the endless horizons no longer exist." — *Science: Endless Horizons or Golden Age?* by Bently Glass (1971)

"Scientists are understandably loath to state publicly that they have entered an era of diminishing returns. No one wants to be recalled as the equivalent of those allegedly shortsighted physicists of a century ago." — *The End of Science* by John Horgan (1996)

"One of the most haunting figures in history is that of the unheeded messenger ... Some lived to see their vindication, some did not. But despite such differences, common virtues emerge: discernment of the times, courage to repudiate powerful interests and fashion, perseverance in the face of daunting odds, seasoned wisdom born of a sense of history and their nation's place in it, and — supremely with the great Hebrew prophets — a ring of conviction in their message born of its transcendent source." — *Unriddling Our Times: Reflections on the Gathering Cultural Crisis*, ed. Os Guinness (2004)

One of the saddest experiences for a community of discourse is for someone (let's call him or her "the prophet") to share knowledge with the group only to be disbelieved and ignored until it is too late to do anything about it. If a community can't mobilize to heed a well-argued warning, then it really has failed as a community of discourse. Perhaps it's a failure of the prophet and the group to form a single community of discourse. The prophet must be an outsider in some sense to have real prescience, but must the prophet be an outsider to the point that he can't communicate his message and the community can't hear it? It's cold comfort for the stoned prophet to say "I told you so."

"Another way to look at this is to make an analogy with AIDS. AIDS does not kill people; it simply destroys the immune system ... The 'violence immune system' exists in the midbrain, and conditioning in the media creates an 'acquired deficiency' in this immune system. With this weakened immune system, the victim becomes more vulnerable to violence-enabling factors, such as poverty, discrimination, drug addiction ... or guns and gangs (which can provide the means and 'support structure' to commit violent acts.)" — *On Killing: The Psychological Cost of Learning to Kill in War and Society* by Lt. Col. Dave Grossman (1996)

When a teacher and four girls were gunned down, and 11 more wounded by a 13 year-old and an 11 year-old in Lt. Col. Dave Grossman's hometown of Jonesboro, Arkansas on March 24,1998, he argued that de facto desensitizing and conditioning of children through violent films and video games made "senseless" shootings chillingly explicable and predictable. He argued that our robust midbrain resistance to killing members of our own species can be bypassed through prolonged desensitization and conditioning. It's a bit circular, but Grossman contends that this reduced resistance makes us (or them) vulnerable to violence-enabling factors. If his AIDS analogy is on target, so to speak, then the research he champions (dubbed "killology") is almost impossible to imagine *without* raising ethical issues. If the scientific assessment of killing rigorously leads us to re-evaluate military history, video games, or terrorism, that would affect many communities of discourse, wouldn't it?

Share No. 10. Scholarship about violence is not exclusively about war and persecution in far away places. Research each of the murders which happened in your community during the past year. Exercise charitable interpretation about stories from newspapers and TV broadcasts. What are witnesses, family members, neighbors, police, and the community trying to explain? How do they interpret these murders? What are the best possible understandings they are trying to convey? Next, write paragraphs about each one of the killings. Don't worry about what "kind" of killing occurred. Simply identify the victim, the killer (if possible), and tell a brief story about what happened and why. Finally, visit the site of one of the murders and meditate at that location for ten minutes. Murders happen to actual people at real places not far from you.

Chapter Two

Principles and Skills of Ethical Argumentation

Introduction. What principles are most relevant to guide critical thinkers in making their arguments sustaining? With our emphasis upon community and mutual respect in sustaining arguments, *cooperation* looks like a promising principle. Certainly, there is enough uncooperative and abusive discourse in the world to make cooperation look very desirable as a guiding principle to govern and guarantee sustaining arguments. Further, we see the value of collaboration in science and other fields. At first glance, it looks sensible to make cooperation our one and only principle to guide ethical argumentation.

However, we could also make a good argument for taking competition as a guiding principle. Truth can be revealed through honest competition as surely as it can be uncovered through cooperation. Though rivalry can be nasty or counter-productive, not all rivalry undermines a community of discourse. It can even be healthy. Therefore, "survival of the fittest" might be too drastic a metaphor for the competition we seek. Let's use a sports metaphor instead. Fierce competition, undertaken according to rules which govern the competition, can foster mutual respect and strengthen a team and the entire sports community, regardless of which team happens to win or lose a particular game.

So, perhaps a fierce debate in ethical argumentation can do the same. Debates don't have to be abusive just because both sides strongly defend their position. When cooperation respects differences on the way to consensus, and when competition doesn't sacrifice respect for rules and competitors to the goal of winning at all costs, both styles of social interaction can guide us to sustaining arguments: arguments which matter, about things which matter, to people who matter to each other.

We need skills of cooperation *and* competition because conflict doesn't just accidentally show up in arguments. It's built-in if you're arguing about anything that really matters (and matters to you). So, be prepared for disagreement on issues, and don't be intimidated or discouraged by disagreement. The fact that you disagree with someone doesn't mean that the two of you have failed to be ethical or nice to each other. It means at least that the principle of substance (see below) is in effect. Conflict in arguments about issues that matter to all parties is *normal* and does not signal failure or license one party abusing the other. Sometimes arguments stride forward. At other junctures, they stall, seem to go backwards or fall apart. Whatever the conflict or the problem, be persistent in your reasoning and learn as a community from your impasses and failures. A "sustaining" argument sustains the community through its own conflicts.

What we need are principles which best guide and promote the features of sustaining arguments. Let's consider the following principles: charity, substance, scholarship, and conflict, and see how they relate to the features of sustaining arguments, You may remember these four principles from the Introduction:

A. Doing Charitable Interpretation by Being Objective. Sustaining arguments respect the intelligence and humanity of the both the arguer and intended audience by helping rather than hindering our ability to think, and by supporting rather than undermining a community of discourse. We can achieve this by applying the **principle of charitable interpretation**: choose the most plausible interpretation of the arguer's words and the best reasoning to be found in those words.[1]

---

1. Why interpret an argument in the best possible light? It's in your self-interest to spare yourself unnecessary confusion. It's kind to treat the

B. *Honoring matters of substance through learning how to suffer:* Sustaining arguments prove something worth discussing, allow questioning decisions worth considering, or lead to commitments worth making. We can achieve this by applying the **principle of substance:** choose only matters and issues for arguments which deserve your best thinking, facilitate necessary decisions, and in which there are stakes that matter for the benefit or detriment of all concerned.

C. *Practicing great scholarship by remaining curious.* Sustaining arguments are also necessarily good arguments which are factually based and logically coherent. We can achieve this by applying the **principle of scholarship:** Acknowledge and deal with the obstacles to knowledge effectively enough to investigate the truth of propositions, test the strength of inferences, and evaluate the merits of an argument.

D. *Handling conflict by seeing when enough is enough.* Sustaining arguments are also arguments which strengthen a community as it confronts and learns from the conflicts, impasses, failures, and sacrifices which are part of arguing together as a community. We can achieve this by applying the **principle of conflict:** Acknowledge that any good argument invites conflict and that the community of discourse is charged with working effectively through the conflicts in its arguments. The community is sustained by the way that it handles its conflicts in argument.

---

argument as tendered in good faith, and you are diligently honoring optimal reasoning by doing so. Those are all good reasons. But it's not ethical practice unless you recognize that we also collaborate in our thinking. That makes charity a mutual obligation and not just a one-way rescue of someone's needy argument. As ethical practice, we apply the principle even more earnestly to arguments which are shoddy, dishonest, or just plain sloppy. Sometimes the least deserving reasoning needs charity the most. That's less gratifying that polishing a good argument into a great one, but we can shame as well as invite each other into a renewed community of discourse.

A. Doing Charitable Interpretation by Being Objective

The principle of charitable interpretation is a fixture of critical thinking. Choose the most plausible interpretation of the arguer's words and the interpretation which honors the best reasoning to be found in those words. To foster arguments which respect the intelligence and humanity of everyone involved and which help instead of hinder argument and discourse, we can adopt *the principle of charitable interpretation*. The principle arises spontaneously, once you get used to the idea that critical thinking is more than wielding a set of formal rules and honing value-neutral skills of argumentation. You start to recognize how the ways in which we practice our thinking, argue together, or try to solve problems can also bring up ethical questions: What virtues does a good critical thinker possess? What values matter most for beginning and continuing critical thinking among people?

As we answer those questions, it makes sense to devote the same care and respect to one person's argument as we would wish to receive for our own arguments. Any argument has both strengths and weaknesses. For this reason, critical thinking *espouses the principle of charitable interpretation*. This means that if an argument, in part or in whole, is subject to more than one interpretation, we choose the most plausible interpretation of the arguer's words. We try to accurately represent the argument, even if we have reasons to criticize the argument or its conclusion.

This caring and careful thinking is clearly more than a rule of logic. It's also a reciprocal ethical agreement to help each other to reason as well as possible. You might think of the principle of charity as an example of the Golden Rule. You take sufficient care to recognize and acknowledge the actual strengths and weaknesses of someone's argument just as you would want that person to give your arguments the same measure of honest consideration. You try to build upon the strengths of another's argument and not dismiss the argument solely because of its perceived weaknesses. You would hope that your arguments can provide the same benefit for others.

What would *uncharitable* interpretation look like? A failure to show such charity is analogous to the phenomenon of "malicious obedience" in a store, factory, or office. When an employee resents a manager's orders or rules, the employee uses this passive-aggressive tactic to do absolutely nothing more than the exact letter of the rules or order, contributing no empathy, intelligent interpretation, accommodation, or charity. It's an effective way to undermine authority. A classic fallacy of reasoning called the "straw man fallacy" in which someone presents a weaker version of an opponent's argument for the sole purpose of knocking it down, is likewise uncharitable interpretation. It's a way to undermine your opponent. Uncharitable interpretation fails to show concern for the ultimate merits of an argument or the well-being of the community of discourse.

"Charitable interpretation" does *not* mean ignoring an argument's weaknesses or presenting the argument as better than it happens to be just to avoid offending the arguer or rocking the community's boat. However, this principle can be effective in helping the argument to evolve and actually become a better argument while sustaining the mutual respect that a community of discourse needs in order to think and argue about anything. It means being diligently and proficiently objective about the argument you hear or read. That will help to keep you or your partner honest about the merits or shortcomings of your critical thinking.

Recommending **objectivity** may come as a shock. Most of us would expect that the principle of charitable interpretation would be most faithfully applied by some sort of subjectivity: wearing the arguer's shoes and learning the arguer's unique perspective thoroughly. Charity seems to point us toward subjectivity or at least intersubjectivity. So, why should learning how to be objective matter to charity?

Think of charity as requiring a particular tough-love skill. Charitable interpretation is a principle for critical thinking which we apply not by pandering to the weaknesses in an argument or giving it the most euphemistic and flattering interpretation possible. It is not an emergency fix to shore up a faltering and pitiable line of reasoning. The principle of charitable interpretation is a commitment to be as honest as possible about the scope and nature of the argument's genuine merits. Honest praise, like honest criticism, requires objectivity too.

We can perform this skill of objectivity well or badly but never perfectly. The perfection we associate with objectivity makes it a philosophical hot potato and associates objectivity with fear of contamination. "Distilled water" may be a better metaphor for objectivity and less of a cliché than "hot potato." If you consider objectivity as bottled distilled water or spring water, it's perfect, pure, and divested of all subjective contaminants. On the other hand, it's also not so dirty or useful as dish water or bath water. A fear-based objectivity mimics ancient purity codes. It banishes pollutants but does no real ethical work and tempts us to infer too quickly that objectivity is out of reach. We might think that therefore *any* intelligent effort to be objective is an exercise in pointless precision (a.k.a., utter futility, impossible dreaming, naïve realism, or mental posturing). We couldn't imagine that aspiring to this elusive objectivity could be charitable or sensible.

Notwithstanding, the choice between having true objectivity or else no objectivity at all may be a false dilemma. We can still usefully think of objectivity as a discipline with moral dimensions. Practicing objectivity demands accommodations to the object of inquiry and taking stock of our own subjectivity. This implies prescriptions and perhaps duties associated with those accommodations and our own biases. Objectivity demands relating to facts in ways which respect them, having the integrity to not subordinate your judgment, and developing the humility and shrewdness to keep your judgment from being compromised by bias and prejudice. We are likely to be more skillfully objective about some subjects than others.

Still, objectivity matters to ethics because it is one important way we respect not only arguments, but also *the people who share them*. Practicing objectivity implies with genuine cognitive sincerity that a person's argument is worth taking seriously, whether you think it's a good argument or not. Objectivity also requires hard work because learning how to be objective *about* a topic means tending to pertinent social biases, carefully handling a topic which provokes strong feelings, broaching a topic which is extremely subjective or personal, or coping with a topic's unfamiliarity, uncertainty, incompleteness, ambiguities, or even paradoxes. And, yes, it means wearing the arguer's shoes for awhile.

Again, as critical thinkers, we aren't equally committed to, or competent at, the skill of objectivity with respect to each and every topic. That's another reason we need to participate in a community of discourse to do critical thinking well. For the topic under consideration, objectivity requires patience, persistence, and an unwillingness to settle for conclusions that do not reflect our best judgment. It's an essential nutrient in a community of discourse in which people respect each other and the topic under consideration. The discipline of objectivity is generic, but the competence is specific.

So, let's not confuse objectivity with what it is not. Objectivity is not adopting an attitude of coolness, detachment, or aloofness. Objectivity is not the absence of emotions. Objectivity is not cultivating the fantasy of being a self-contained subject who is entirely independent of whatever one investigates. Objectivity is not the delusion that whatever we select for our objective attention is thereby genuinely isolated *in vitro*, disconnected with everything that it's contingent upon. Objectivity is not pretending that we stand outside the world and look at it through a perfectly transparent window. Let's not waste time defining objectivity in ways which aren't honest about how interdependent we are with anything we take as an object.

In ethics, objectivity is a skill that doesn't quite rise to the level of virtue. It is useful, desirable, and even admirable, where it is appropriate or even possible, but it doesn't seem deeply attached to moral character. People may be grateful for your objectivity, but it's your honesty that they eulogize. Objectivity is more accurately an ethical skill or discipline. We expect a good judge to be objective but, ethically speaking, we expect much more as well. Don't flaunt objectivity as a sterling virtue which makes subjectivity into a shameful vice. A good surgeon who is objective about surgery isn't therefore morally entitled to ignore the patient's (subjective) pain. Objectivity is an important ethical discipline, but it's not a bona fide virtue, much less a redeeming virtue.

In school, you might describe objective tests as containing true/false, multiple choice, or fill-in-the-blank questions. You might describe objective vocations as those which are primarily evidence-centered (such as diagnostic or forensic medicine). But practicing objectivity is not limited to obviously evidence-grounded vocations. **It means learning and respecting how *what* we know disciplines *how* we know it.** It doesn't deny our interdependence with what we know, but is astute about what kind of relationship with what we know that is optimal. Practicing objectivity balances the practice of curiosity.

Share No. 11 It can be easier to champion objectivity than to find a home for it. Imagine that you overhear an impassioned argument about whether American citizens, regardless of their political beliefs, should always support U.S. soldiers in combat. You intervene and state that you are in a position to be objective about this contentious issue, because you have diligently researched American combat activity and policy. You have listened carefully intelligently to differing points of view on this issue and have considered them carefully. You've spoken to peace activists, veterans, politicians about this and have found out how innocent citizens endangered by this combat deal with the situation. The debaters are impressed until you mention that your brother is a combat soldier, and that this motivated you to become interested in finding out all about American combat activity and policies. The arguers object that your family involvement means that you have no objectivity about this topic.

How do you respond? Do you meekly agree that you are not emotionally detached and therefore can't be objective? Do you defiantly assert that, notwithstanding your brother, your arguments should be judged solely on their own merits? Do you re-emphasize that your brother's danger makes you uniquely motivated and committed to thinking about this topic? Do you discredit the arguers for being too personally isolated from combat realities to have any credibility? Does objectivity have a home in your research on this issue? Before you write a three-page essay answering these questions, listen at length to someone who has a sibling in combat. Think about their response. Then write and share your answers with others.

Share No. 12 Imagine that you're swimming in the Gulf of Mexico and a pod of dolphins swims in your direction. With what you take as reasonable objectivity, you conclude that the dolphins are friendly towards you. But are they *really* friendly or are you anthropomorphizing their relationship to you? Perhaps the shape of their skulls only make these 300–500 pound wild animals look like they're smiling and therefore friendly. Maybe they are bored and just curious about you, especially if they haven't encountered humans in general or you in particular. How would you assess their friendliness objectively? Come up with an objective standard for identifying friendly dolphins. Identify the most likely ways in which you could be wrong. Don't try an inventory of each and every conceivable error you could make. Based on your research, identify counterfeits: the most likely dolphin behaviors which would resemble friendliness but would actually express different motives and goals. In two pages, state your standard of objectivity for assessing friendliness and the most probably ways in which it might be mistaken.

Next, imagine that you are a mature dolphin in the Gulf of Mexico, at least 20 years old, and that your pod echo-locates a swimming human nearby. You've never encountered a human before. As you swim closer, the human flails about casually in the water without attacking. The human is humming something which catches your attention but makes no sounds that you can understand. Is this swimmer a friendly animal? It does not swim towards you or your pod. Would you allow the calves (younger dolphins) to swim any nearer to the human? How would you and the other dolphins safely and objectively assess the friendliness of this human swimmer? How is it possible that you could be mistaken about its friendliness? In two pages, state your standard of objectivity for assessing friendliness and the most probably ways in which it might be mistaken.

Share No. 13. A journalist decides to write a story for her magazine on how Hurricane Katrina affected people on the Gulf Coast who remained during the disaster in New Orleans, Pascagoula, Ocean Springs, and Long Beach during August 2005. She interviews people in different locales and vocations about their losses, fears, and why they did not or could not leave the area. She charitably interprets the responses of her mumbling, exhausted, and flustered interviewees. The editor objects that the journalist did not interview the higher income people who buy and read the magazine. The journalist points out that the rich were able to evacuate the coast and have not returned. The editor responds that the story is unbalanced because it presents only one group's perspective and also distorts the public's perception of an area that is trying to recover economically.

As a skill for applying the principle of charity, we noted that objectivity means learning and respecting how what we know disciplines how we know it. A sudden disaster disciplines how we come to know that disaster in certain ways. Disasters call forth charity in many senses, but it also obstructs urgently needed help. For example, the reporter hopes that publicity will help, even though she is primarily a voyeur of the calamity. Disasters also demand ethical choices while disrupting the social, economic, and personal relationships upon which we rely for extending charity. For example, do the secure journalist and the insecure interviewees have a truly ethical relationship with each other? If the interviewee scrounges for food, is he objectively a resourceful survivor, a looter, an inspiring survivor, a reason for more police, an unheard voice of the dispossessed, or someone too engulfed by chaos and loss to understand the disaster? Encountering someone who has been yanked out of routine into stark isolation disciplines how you report that person. Objectively, we respect how the disaster shapes our knowing while taking responsibility for the ways in which we know. Do some research of news accounts of a recent disaster in which a range of people are interviewed about what happened and what it meant. In a three-page essay, indicate the ways in which the reporting succeeds or fails to be objective. The question isn't whether the interviewees are objective, but whether the news story shows any skill of objectivity.

Share No. 14 This may seem like an easy share to research. For an hour, baby-sit a child who is four years old or younger and write the most objective three-page essay about this child that you can manage. Pick any topic about the child that interests you. You needn't be dispassionate, detached, or exclusively descriptive to do this. However, the child may want to play with you. You might like or resent the child. Keep writing. The child wants to know what you're writing about. If you tell the child, does that make your report less objective? Would a psychologist, doctor, parent, or another child agree that your report is objective? First, be able to explain what you mean by being "objective" about the topic you chose. You do want to share more than your opinions and biases.[2]

---

2. Werner Heisenberg's uncertainty principle in quantum mechanics developed in the 1920's, has been generalized to make objectivity seem impossible. Heisenberg argued that the more precisely the position of a particle is determined, the less precisely the momentum is known. We may observe passively or actively, but *any* observation interacts with and alters what we observe. Still, this very interaction is at the core of objectivity as an ethical skill. We both allow the observed to discipline how we know it *and* we hold ourselves accountable for how we know it. The observed particle is no mere artifact of our observation, nor are we inert clay (*parce*

B. Honoring Matters of Substance through Learning How to Suffer

Choose only matters and issues for arguments which deserve your best thinking, facilitate necessary decisions, and in which there are stakes that matter for the benefit or detriment of all concerned. This principle is a guide to choosing what is worth arguing about. A good analogy would be making nutritional dietary choices. People can and do eat and drink a wide variety of things, but not all dietary choices are equally nutritional. If we push this analogy a bit further, we'd have to ask which arguments are simply "junk food." Some arguments may be not just poorly constructed but unhealthy or even toxic. As we sort through arguments to find the sustaining ones, here are a few samples of arguments lacking substance which are not likely to make the cut:

When people argue primarily to attack each other, defend themselves, or to make a complaint, then it's unlikely that any real decision or commitment will emerge from such arguments. The social purpose of these arguments is not primarily to reason with others. Such an argument might be emotionally gratifying or even technically strong, but it doesn't have much value for the participants' thinking about issues that matter. Call them *"ulterior motive" arguments.*

When people argue about matters which no amount of reasonable investigation or shared experience can be expected to settle, then no argument of substance results. Call these *exercises "dark side of the moon" arguments.* The more responsible way to approach these topics would be agree to speculate about the topic or to fig-

---

Locke) molded by what we observe. We're in *relationship* with the observed. Therefore, ethics is no longer optional for critical thinking, and objectivity on these terms is a form of respect.

ure out some way to further investigate. The topic simply isn't ready yet for inference or conclusions.

When people argue about matters in which they have no stake, interest, or experience, we call these exercises *"idle arguments."* We could imagine for any idle argument that, in the right hands and with the right motives, it could become someone's burning issue. However, when the same argument is advanced without any risk or stakes, the argument fails to sustain thinking or a community of discourse in which it is offered.

As a philosopher, I should dispense a "Surgeon General's Warning"[3] at this point. Academic philosophers are sometimes accused of ignoring the principle of substance. They've been blamed for pursuing arguments don't seem to lead to any decisions, which are impervious to any conceivable evidence, and which don't reveal any real living passions or conflicts that would prompt serious thinking. Those are pretty harsh accusations about philosophy lacking substance.

Still, philosophy at its best has always strived for sustaining arguments. Because its arguments are abstract, they appear insubstantial. Because its arguments throughout history are continually superseded by new contending arguments, they appear futile, but that's because the substantial themes of philosophy involving the human condition are so compelling that they can generate new arguments for each generation of thinkers. Be careful not to judge an argument as insubstantial merely because it is initially difficult to follow or doesn't immediately connect with your personal interests.

What about theological arguments? A skeptic might think that theologians disputing matters of faith violate the principle of sub-

---

3. The Surgeon General of the United States is the head of the United States Public Health Service Commissioned Corps. In this office, the Surgeon General is a spokesperson about public health matters. Americans are most familiar with a series of Surgeon General warnings about the dangers of smoking. These are printed in bold letters on cigarette packages in the United States.

stance because their debates can't be settled by empirical investigation. If you're religious enough to feel defensive about this accusation, then imagine overhearing a group of people soberly debating UFO abductions or some metaphysical cult. You might react with the same sort of skepticism and demand empirical evidence. From time to time, we find ourselves on the outside of a community debating matters which are not only of no interest to us, but which we can't even charitably imagine to be worth *anyone's* time. In those situations, do take time to find out what sort of standards (if any) the community upholds for its discourse. Theology, for example, has centuries of tradition examining the logic, shared experience, and institutional traditions of certain beliefs. Because religion and faith are lived out in community, its beliefs do therefore have substantial import for believers' lives.

So, even if you don't share a community's assumptions about what is real or ultimately true, learn whether the community does honor the principle of substance through shared standards. If a scriptural literalist shows scriptural illiteracy, you have cause to criticize the literalist, whether you take the scriptures literally or not.

Yes, here's that calorie-challenged puppy again. An insulting quip attributed to a British MP, Lyndon Johnson, and others is: *"He has all the qualities of a dog except loyalty."* Is that an ethical insult to dogs or to humans? When we assume that humans match or exceed the spiritual depth of canine devotion, are we really making an argument of substance? Perhaps we accept our human ethical superiority on faith because we can talk. But the virtue of loyalty doesn't require many words, does it?

A sensible student might make a relativist objection at this point to this analogy between arguments of substance and good nutrition. After all, dietary knowledge is a matter of health science and can be proven. But who is so authoritative as to declare whether any given argument has substance?

The objection is well-taken if you're confronting a group that wants to preclude any challenge to its priorities by declaring new topics "insubstantial" or "irrelevant" to its status quo. The community assumes that it has already figured out its real needs or that those needs have not changed. The assumption may not be justified. (The following section on suffering suggests why there may not be a general guideline or template for defining "substance.") Applying the principle of substance doesn't define "substance" for all occasions. The principle shouldn't let us pretend that we have already proven the truth of our assumptions about what topics are most important in life or even most important to a community. So, where do we start?

We start wherever we happen to find ourselves. Frankly, one of the ways in which a community starts to constitute itself is by figuring out just what its common needs and interests are or should be. That's not an easy task, nor is it completed once and for all times. Part of this process is for people to sort out which arguments are worth their time and energy and which are not. That doesn't mean that each and every community of discourse would wind up with the same short list of sustaining arguments, but it does imply that a community of discourse should work towards consensus about what is worthwhile to think about together. To return to our nutrition analogy, if a community's discourse turns increasingly sickly, unenergetic, or else feverish and agitated, then, whatever "substance" is for that community, it plainly lacks an essential nutrient. We can then avoid wasteful or toxic conversation even if we don't solve the philosophical or theological question of ultimate value or true substance.

"We mourn the loss of rain forests and timberlands; we watch helplessly as urban sprawl encroaches on meadows and prairies ... but the rampant destruction

of the ocean floor and its endemic fauna is one of the greatest environmental disasters in history, and it is occurring virtually unnoticed. Hidden even from the eyes of those perpetrating the horror, the inhabitants of the ocean floor and the ocean floor itself are being demolished at a rate that defies comprehension." — *The Empty Ocean* (2003) by Richard Ellis

If you are trying to make an argument that your audience hasn't yet recognized as substantial, you may be initially dismissed as alarmist. For example, the bottom of the ocean is, for many of us, a metaphor for irrelevance. It's a place we picture as utterly removed from any vital concerns we may have. That's a challenge for Dr. Ellis, isn't it? Perhaps that's why we imagine Santa Claus living at the North Pole. That's about as far away as our earth-bound imaginations take us. However, the United States, Denmark, Russia, and Canada want to drill for oil around the North Pole. We will have a hard time finding another suitable "nowhere" anywhere on earth to relocate Santa's shop.

Share No. 15 Matters far removed in time or distance may not receive fair and sufficient consideration by your community in doing scholarship or deciding what's substantive either because we don't think such matters count, or we're embarrassed to suggest that they might. Members of minorities who voice their concerns to the community sometimes feel like they are speaking "from the bottom of the ocean" so far as the majority is concerned. Not exactly invisible but virtually labeled as irrelevant or self-contained. Begin a group discussion on date-rape. If you are female, ensure that you are the only woman in the group. If you are male, ensure that you are the only man in the group. Do your best to do a sustaining discussion of this issue. Record the conversation (with the group's permission) and type up the transcript, keeping the identities anonymous (except for you.) Let an outside group decide how well this community of discourse handled the issue, the conflicts, and charitable interpretation. Report the results.

Let's return to the argument that substantial arguments are analogous to good nutrition. Your Author hoped to bury the vampire of relativism successfully with that analogy, but it might have been too shallow a grave. Relativism may rise again. Do we have any non-arbitrary much less absolute consensus on what's worth thinking about together? What binding standard could ward off this defiantly diffident creature of the night? The vampire, partial to quite a different notion of good nutrition than ours, reminds us that "good nutrition" includes a huge menu of possible foods. Even a rigorous diet has room for pretty subjective decisions. A community hungry for good nutrition could therefore disagree in good faith about what to eat. Who's to say that one argument is more nutritious than another? There's room for individuality about matters of taste. Right? Think fast. The vampire's next argument is that you might make a good and tasty meal. That's his truth, and who are we to impose our judgment upon him?

Keep moving! Fortunately, you have the powerful charm of genuine needs to wield. You intone to the vampire that a substantial argument, like good nutrition, may satisfy certain of your genuine needs, and the topic of substance which your (non-vampire) community upheld meets certain of its needs. Undeterred, however, the vampire asks you to consider that the possibility that an argument's value may have nothing to do with whatever needs your community happens to find urgent. Who's to say? Who are YOU to say? I hope you haven't stopped backing away as you ponder this query.

I don't know that we can drive a stake through the heart of relativism to keep it from stalking us further as we collaborate on what's worth our critical thinking. But we might be able to slow it down. Relativism can tempt us to be a bit lazy if it means we needn't bother supporting our own arguments or find out why others argue as they do ("Who's to say?"). It may also make us cynical if it keeps us from investing any trust or sincere interest in why people differ or how they might reconcile their differences. Saying "That's true for you but not for me" or "it's a matter of opinion" without having to care about where the opinions come from, what they mean, or which one should belong to you, is only going to isolate us from each other further. By the way, our blood-sucker likes isolated targets too.

A relativist is not necessarily wiser than a naïve or ignorant thinker, but he or she may be more sophisticated. It's no surprise that the classic vampire is a demonic aristocrat. Relativism has plenty of smug superiority behind its veneer of tolerance. Still, in a world full of hate, doesn't even a veneer of toleration count as moral improvement compared with our sorry history of persecuting and killing people who disagree with us? Sure, the vampire kills too, but it's nothing personal. It's just (for lack of a better phrase) an "inconvenient truth."

Okay, enough of the vampire jokes at the expense of relativism. Seriously, is relativism the best and most responsible response we can come up with when trying to decide what's worth thinking about with others? As a relativist, you may ask rhetorically "*Who's to say* what's substantial?" Of course, you aren't really asking for someone's name. It's a rhetorical question because you assume that no one could have decisive authority about whether any argument is substantial or relevant. If we can't deal honestly with this sort of relativism, then we can't expect a community of discourse to ever agree upon or *explain* how they agree upon a topic satisfying the principle of substance.

If you hold your hand over a flame without flinching, is the trick not to mind the flame or to be especially mindful of it? This brings us to the skill of suffering. Having pain requires no special talent. Bearing pain can be learned to some extent. We can adopt stances towards pain such as stoicism, resistance, resignation, fear, patience, and so forth. So, when does a stance become a skill? To suffer well means that you know enough about what can happen to human beings, and what has and does happen to all of us, that you can live through and with it and remain human. You may not be at your best when in pain, but you can remain human and maybe even become more human. Some faith traditions (notably Buddhist) strongly emphasize this feature of our humanity, but it's also a feature important to the ethics within critical thinking.

This may be one protective charm that the vampire can't overcome. One of the ways we remain human is by suffering with others. It's difficult to do this with grace and completeness by oneself. Isolated suffering easily devolves into worrying, whining, or self-pity. That's analogous to how thinking by oneself can devolve into arguing in circles. Knowing what counts as substantial for a community of discourse is knowing what problem, concern, question, or issue is causing the most hurt or discomfort. We may shy away from facing certain suffering, but doing this capably can be a good test of substance.

Lest we make a fetish of suffering, it's worth noting that people can do their best thinking together when they're enthusiastic, playful, or competitive. Where's the suffering in all that? If people are human enough to suffer, they are human enough to have fun. Without the suffering, they seek out fun, not for its own sake, but to remind themselves that they're human. It forces fun to do work, and, even worse, it gives fun a bad name. It comes up with fun that makes us act less rather than more completely human.

If something does not bother us enough to bother with it, then we're not likely to think. We may suffer under a stick or in chasing a carrot, but complacency doesn't deliver any appreciation of substance. We need enough comfort to think but not so much as to make thinking too comfortable.

You may have heard friends debating some ethical issues that involve real human suffering and making arguments pro or con. However, if they have not suffered through the pertinent circumstances (not just being hurt but developing a skill of dealing with exactly the suffering that give rise to that issue), the arguments risk remaining glib or detached from the real circumstances that create the issue. An argument which is superficial or unconnected to people's lives is not likely to be substantial. We can be well informed about an ethical issue without having much sense of which arguments would be substantial for thinking about that issue. A good argument may not be grim, but does deserve some finesse in dealing with grim realities.

American society doesn't make competent or experienced suffering easy to come by. Not many of us would sign up for that kind of training. If you're sufficiently well-off to presume that life won't hurt very much or for very long, then suffering for you is mostly a real-but-pretty-abstract possibility, isn't it? If we do get hurt, we depend on some quick assistance to lessen the pain and the suffering. We tend to shut suffering people away and out of sight. You might not want to change that way of lessening suffering, but the price is that we don't develop much skill in living with hurt to help us spot what is substantial in our thinking and what is not. We can wind up becoming both naïve AND cynical—ignorant of what hurting does and means and unwilling to trust anyone around us to have any credibility about matters of substance.

Share No. 16 Go to a local car dealership and shop for a vehicle. Decide what type of car you would like to purchase and find out what you can about it. Visit the dealership during the day on a weekday when the lot is not busy. Explain that you're interested in looking at a vehicle although you probably can't afford it at the moment (true enough). Listen carefully to what the salesperson tells you about the automobile and how this person answers your questions. Finally, ask the salesperson where he or she bought their first vehicle. Find out how the purchase went—was this person satisfied or angry with the result? Find out the worst automotive purchase they ever made. What did they learn from that fiasco? Who is the worst customer they've ever encountered and why? Based on what you hear, do you think this sales person has developed the skill of suffering through auto sales sufficiently to know what is substantial in negotiating a sale and what is not? Write this up in a three-page essay and share it with another student and a car salesperson.

C. Practicing Great Scholarship by Remaining Curious

Let's say that the principle of scholarship is to acknowledge and deal with the obstacles to knowledge effectively enough to investigate the truth of proposition, test the strength of inferences, and evaluate the merits of an argument. It's not very kind for someone to tell you to go "get the facts" as if you were a child running to pick up sea shells. Even a child with high-speed Internet access will find that facts needed for an argument aren't strewn about on the beach pre-labeled as "true" or "false." Scholarship is less a stroll along the surf than an obstacle course through unknown and possibly hostile territory. The hard work is figuring out what assertions or claims can be trusted enough to count as facts.

It gets worse. Even information you've determined to be reasonably trustworthy and reliable still needs to be interpreted as you think through its logical implications, its relationship to other information you have, and its application to issues which matter. You are then in a better position to decide which pertinent facts are still missing and which facts are still needed. Also, we can expect that, if the argument is about a new or controversial subject, then the facts we need may be hidden or disputed. For this reason, we need at least one more principle. Call it *"the principle of scholarship."* This is not a cynical and indiscriminate mistrust of what we hear and see, but a shrewd and diligent set of disciplines and skills for investigating and assessing all sources of information with an aim of working with a community for the sake of more trustworthy knowledge.

We further need a principle of scholarship because, whether we look for facts in our immediate surroundings, or in books, newspapers, or the Internet, facts can be suppressed, slanted, deleted, or taken out of context. Again, it's not cynicism to recognize that, even when we don't encounter outright lies and falsehood, information resources which are controlled by one or only a few persons or corporations, or which are offered solely to sell products or services are not likely to be objective or impartial about what they offer. In order for us to be scholars as well as critical thinkers, we need to face such a situation honestly, shrewdly, and imaginatively. We also have to admit that we unconsciously ignore or dismiss unfamiliar facts that don't comfortably fit inside the boundaries of our perspective or conform to our past experience.

While we're being so diligent about sorting, sifting, and scrutinizing what counts as a "fact," scholarship doesn't end there. We're also seeking and judging what counts as a good argument. Unfortunately, extended and well-reasoned arguments do not often appear in the media or in popular print media. More often, we encounter sound bites, retorts, dumbed-down prose, and snippets of news without context. It may be that philosophers complain about this more than most people, but do you think we have plenty of daily exposure to sustaining or even thoughtful arguments? Perhaps instead of complaining, we should see this as a golden opportunity to introduce as many good and sustaining arguments as we wish. But first we have to be scholarly enough to know where they're present, missing, or needed.

Cynicism may creep in again at this point. Should we spurn or suspect any argument offered by someone who is arguing to make money? Isn't that an "ulterior motive?" No, it's not ulterior unless the argument lacks substance for the community in question. Marketing and business majors don't need to renounce their chosen professions as devoid of trustworthy facts or good faith arguments. Whether you argue to buy or sell, you rely quite a bit on the trustworthiness or at least the perceived trustworthiness of your arguments and your own reputation as part of earning a living.

In fact, we learn to apply the principles of charity and scholarship in the media and in business. Whether we're consumers or doing our job, we need to find a representative sample of pertinent perspectives, check for inconsistencies, and collaborate to make full use our life experiences to test the trustworthiness of what we take to be facts. It's not easy to be discerning about this. Just think of cynicism here as a lazy and indiscriminate rejection of an argument without considering its real merits. Instead, apply the same principle of scholarship and you may find some arguments that are first-rate and can be models to emulate for making new arguments. In this way, even arguments that don't make money for anyone can nevertheless have a pay-off!

How do you apply the principle of scholarship in your own community of discourse? Here are some suggestions:

1. Do your homework and learn the facts, but realize that the facts are not necessarily pre-identified and pre-verified for your convenience. Be aware that your own perspective may blind or bias you as to which facts you manage to notice or even which experiences you're willing to regard as facts. Be open-minded as well as diligent.

2. Get to know each other's backgrounds in your community of discourse. Whenever you do scholarship, you're not only learning, but you're teaching others. Being a good scholar means taking responsibility not just for what you learn but for how you can best share that knowledge with others.

3. Remember that there is more than one way to do scholarship. Although much of scholarship is discovering and testing facts, scholarship is also about pulling facts together into new and meaningful patterns as you discover how facts relate to each other. Scholarship happens as you apply what you learn to daily life or teach others. Sometimes scholarship is "research" in the academic sense. At other times, it looks more like networking, brainstorming, and getting the big picture.

For example, I help to lead a church youth group. The leaders wanted to find out who in the group of a dozen 14–15 year-old girls and boys has leadership qualities. We could have handed out personality inventories and scored them. That would be analogous to academic scholarship. But instead, we went on a challenge course together, swinging on ropes, balancing on logs, and hoisting and yanking each other up and over a 11½ foot wall. (In the absence of photos, you'll just have to visualize that spectacle for yourself.) This particular bit of extreme scholarship rather reliably manifested leadership qualities in a number of the teenagers.

In *The Nichomachean Ethics* and *The Posterior Analytics*, Aristotle identifies a number of intellectual virtues which he classifies as theoretical, practical, or productive. For example, there's the virtue of deliberating well, being prudent, or even being wise. You can have the intellectual virtue of good judgment and perhaps courageous judgment. You can be admired for understanding or cleverness. At this point, it would be handy to have Socrates interject and demand, "What makes these things all virtues?" After all, how many (or any) moral virtues does critical thinking really require?

If we shift from identifying ethical virtues to instead identifying ethical skills, we'll think less about our ethical credentials and more about our ethical abilities. That will help us to be good scholars. Critical thinking in scholarship requires us to apply certain skills persistently, dynamically, and usefully in a community of discourse as we encounter detours, impasses, and sudden opportunities for understanding. Why not focus upon virtues? Well, though virtues (such as honesty, bravery, or fairness) are displayed in action and in context just as skills are, it's tempting to consider virtues as virtually self-contained entities, sort of like scouting merit badges. Collecting them can leave us indefinitely begging the question about any ethical competence we might need.

A key skill for critical thinking which Aristotle, Kant, and other philosophers speak less about is *curiosity*. Curiosity is not just an unsatisfied desire for particular information. That sort of frustration may lead us to give up on seeking the unavailable information. However, your frustration becomes true curiosity when you nurture and act upon your thirst, craving, or desire to learn or know things, particularly by successfully overcoming obstacles to finding out. Since you can exercise curiosity well or clumsily, it can be sustained skillfully or not. It can also atrophy if it's not developed.

For example, dolphins are mammals which can sleep without

drowning. You may not know why. You may have a theory or an idea of how to find out. *But,* if you're not curious about that, you immediately or eventually shrug your shoulders and say "somehow." But, if you wonder at all, you then have a discipline of wonder to cultivate. Who would you ask? Where would you look? How would you figure this out? With discipline and dedication, the otherwise idle curiosity becomes a powerful skill. Not knowing becomes not just frustrating but intolerable.

The skill of curiosity may be more important to knowledge than those old we-have-arrived favorites of epistemology: *understanding and believing.* In fact, you have to wonder if the holy grail of true knowledge is desirable if it took no curiosity to get there. It is difficult to imagine healthy critical thinking without it.

Does curiosity kill the cat? On the contrary, when we subtract curiosity from the cat, scarcely a feline remains. No, whoever kills curiosity itself is much more lethal to epistemology, no matter how much or how little we might think we know. Knowledge *without* curiosity is what you get when a class learns about history only by watching TV documentaries. You and your classmates may be informed, but, if you aren't really curious about history, you only warehouse video data. You haven't done any critical thinking about history. Aren't you the least bit curious? How badly do you want to know? Well, the answer may be "no" and "not much," respectively. To switch metaphors, when your curiosity is a sleeping dolphin, you risk drowning either from not enough or too much information.

For example, if you join a team of other engineers to figure out why a space shuttle exploded, would you want a team, no matter how smart, without curiosity? A curious person spots situations which do not make sense and doesn't tolerate them *not* making sense. A curious person doesn't romanticize mysteries and puzzles. A mystery which invites no curiosity is a boring mystery. A puzzle which courts no curiosity is a pointless puzzle.

Ethically speaking, curiosity is somewhat problematic. At the very least, we send children mixed messages about whether curiosity is a good thing. Think of the venerable "Highlights for Children" icons, Goofus and Gallant. In those comic moral lessons, does Gallant ever show *any* curiosity? Nosey characters are the ones who get children's stories moving, but they usually suffer for their initiative. Perhaps the adult message is not just that curiosity has a cost, but that it disrespects discretion, accommodation, manners, and (occasionally) morals. Curiosity doesn't mind its own business. Still, like any discipline, curiosity can be performed clumsily or with investigative adroitness. It's a uniquely subjective bootstrap-discipline because it based upon a desire which must sustain itself and direct itself, and a community somehow helps this to happen.

Keeping curiosity alive in a group means keeping wonder alive and directed, preferably not in asocial ways. Keeping that direction is work, because curiosity is easily distracted and because, without a shared direction, it can devolve into "idle" curiosity which simply consumes ready-made gossip or novel information and seeks to know without incurring any cost or accountability for poking around.

Share No. 17 I choose not to own a cell phone. People routinely use cell phones in public. As a bystander, you can't hear the other side of the conversation, so you may be curious. You can't help listening not just because of sound, but because you want to fill in the blanks. Your curiosity is being provoked and is not being respected. There's no easy way to satisfy it. If people could use cell phones silently (or with speaker phones), you'd either hear nothing or everything—and be less curious. Of course, the other side of the conversation may be none of your business, but then why are you expected to put up with listening to any of it? Don't use your cell phone in public for a full day *unless* you first ask anyone who can hear you whether the conversation will annoy them. If they say "yes," don't use your phone. You may ask in any fashion you choose, but you must solicit permission to interrupt the space around you with your otherwise private phone conversation. Report the results. How did it feel for you, how did others react, how did it work?

Share No. 18 For a full day, whenever you hear someone use a cell phone around you, politely point out to them that it is annoying and ask that they seek talking or else go elsewhere to continue the conversation. If this happens in a restaurant, complain to the management. However, if the person you speak to asks your permission to continue the conversation, you may decide whether or not to consent. Report the results.

Share No. 19. At least once today, interrupt someone using their cell phone in public and ask them questions about who they're talking with or the topic of conversation. Be friendly about it. Join in the conversation just as if you walked up to two of your friends who happened to be conversing with each other. After all, if the person using the cell phone wanted a private conversation, they would have stayed in their room, right?? Be inquisitive. Be snoopy. Take out your cell phone and involve that person standing next to you in your phone conversation too. Report the results.

We expect strange or bizarre things to provoke curiosity. But if our curiosity is hostage to oddities, then it will take constant novelty to sustain curiosity. We can be curious about ordinary things too. These are things which surprise us by revealing our own "curiosity receptors." You may not be curious about why your little brother or sister can stand on one foot with eyes closed much longer than you can. One challenge to provoking and sustaining useful curiosity in a group is that we aren't curious about the same things or equally prepared to be snoopy. One curious person in a group is not enough. You need at least two. A lone curious person can be dismissed as a fool. Two curious people can tag-team a group into a curiosity shop. For example, your group wants to understand why so many new business enterprises fail. Of course, they don't want their own businesses to fail. They may be concerned for others. They may think there are many causes. They are frustrated. *But are they curious?*

Share No. 20 Write a dialog with three people who are talking about this subject of why businesses fail. You can decide which sort of business field the five are discussing. The characters in your dialog will come up with all sorts of explanations: lack of experience, lack of capital, government regulations, unfair competition, and so forth. Now, two new characters enter the conversation and are genuinely puzzled about why all these business bankruptcies are happening. What sort of things would these curious arrivals ask or say? They won't take "no" or "I don't know" for an answer. Would they be interesting, annoying, obnoxious, or intriguing? How would the other characters react?

Share No. 21 In an earlier era, children learned scholarship by looking up facts in an encyclopedia. The Internet hasn't driven multi-volume A–Z encyclopedias to extinction just yet. Rather, this durable reference staple has evolved in unexpected ways. What kind of scholarship are you doing when you quote and not just cut-and-paste information from an encyclopedia? In the 18th century, French philosophes Diderot and d'Alembert undertook the massive encyclopedia of human knowledge. You may get a sample of this undertaking by perusing this online resource: http://quod.lib.umich.edu/d/did/.

In our time, Wikipedia has become the Internet's version of the old encyclopedia but with new cyber dynamics in how it grows. Quoting Wikipedia is debatable scholarship. Wiki has a wide array of sources and contributors but you may not know the worth or depth of their expertise, or how unbiased they are in articles about controversial subjects. Read about its scope and history (naturally) at this Wiki site: http://en.wikipedia.org/wiki/Wikipedia:About.

For the future, the Encyclopedia of Life at http://www.eol.org/ may be the most important mammoth reference work. Find out its scope and purpose, who makes it possible, and estimate how long it will take to complete it for all 1.8 million species. By the time it's finished, many of those species may be extinct. Compare these three encyclopedias as foundations of scholarship in their eras. Each of them strives to be comprehensive, credible, and eventually authoritative. Explain how you'd apply the Principle of Scholarship to citing any of these encyclopedias, and describe what kind(s) of credibility each one has in its era.

D. Handling Conflict by Seeing When Enough Is Enough

We can devise a *principle of conflict*: Let's acknowledge that any good argument invites conflict and that the community of discourse is charged with working effectively through the conflicts in its arguments. The community is sustained by the way that it handles its conflicts in argument.

This principle shouldn't come as a complete surprise. It follows from the first three. If you apply the principle of charity to argue in good faith, then, once you have established each other's positions, you'll discover conflicts. Likewise, if you really apply the principle of substance and argue about matters you care about, then people will care enough to voice opposition. Although our principle of scholarship might settle some conflicts about matters of fact or evidence, new evidence could just as easily unearth unexpected conflicts.

Therefore, conflict is not an external incursion into sustaining arguments. Conflict does not crawl out from under a rock or arrive from outer space. It develops directly from applying principles of charity, substance, and scholarship. But isn't conflict the very thing that threatens to tear apart a community of discourse? How can it be sustaining? We learn to skillfully expect conflicts, handle them well, and accept that arguments that matter will be bumpy and risky. In fact, if we apply this principle of conflict well, our community might justifiably argue more confidently and become confident enough to risk other conflicts in its future arguments.

Arguments that appear in textbooks as examples and exemplars of good SAT-quality reasoning, tend to plod forward soberly, prudently, and sometimes eloquently to balanced and judiciously-supported conclusions. Arguments which appear in communities also march forward at times, but they also hit road blocks. At those junctures, mediation and compromise might be enough to get things moving again. However, the argument may continue to stall, and even seem to retreat when evidence surfaces that casts doubt upon its propositions, or else fall apart, forcing the community to pick up the pieces and try again with better arguments or simply new arguments. These disruptions reveal conflicts which the community needs to face. Though a community of discourse may initially address conflicts by smoothing them over for the sake of continuing the discussion, conflicts have a way of eventually calling attention to themselves. When they're ignored too long, they undermine the discourse and the community.

To put it bluntly, people in a community may find it difficult to pursue an argument because they hate each other's guts, and possibly for good reasons. If the animosity has hardened and deepened over time, the real challenge will be for these bitter enemies to imagine themselves as belonging to the same community of *discourse*. To the outsider, this stand-off appears utterly hopeless. Any aspiration to form a sustaining community of discourse seems laughably idealistic and futile. Indeed, these opponents now practically define themselves by their own feud.

Are you thinking about the Middle East? Think instead about having to cooperate with an ex-boyfriend or ex-girlfriend. Think of family gatherings ruined by one or more very unhappy relatives with grudges. The hurt has become their identity. And yet ... both sides need to heal their wounds. Both sides need to figure out how to form a future in which they manage to co-exist. Both sides may, in fact, have a great deal in common although they are fiercely opposed on one particular issue or some past incident which, by mutual consent, forbids community. If blithely joining hands seems unrealistic, it's not nearly so unrealistic as continuing to sacrifice the future's possibilities to past hatreds.

Conflict is to be expected, and, if we handle it well, even the worst conflict can be an opportunity for growth. If we can't handle them, then they can destroy all possibility of discourse. It's a difficult dynamic involving two resources not often summoned in the name of critical thinking: apology and forgiveness. The conflict may be within a small group or part of a larger and more serious conflict. For example, Archbishop Desmond Tutu, former Chairman of the Truth and Reconciliation Commission in South Africa, speaks of how the white minority and the black majority handled conflict after many years of the oppressive apartheid system. He observed in *No Future Without Forgiveness:*

"There may indeed have been moments when God may have regretted creating us. But I am certain there have been many more times when God has looked and seen all these wonderful people who have shone in the dark night of evil and torture and abuses and suffering; shone as they have demonstrated their nobility of spirit, their magnanimity as they have been ready to forgive, and so they have dispelled the murkiness, and fresh air has blown into that situation to transfigure it. It has filled people with new hope that despair, darkness, anger and resentment and hatred would not have the last word. There is hope that a new situation could come about when enemies might become friends again, when the dehumanized perpetrator might be helped to recover his lost humanity. This is not a wild irresponsible dream. It has happened and it is happening and there is hope that nightmares will end, hope that seemingly intractable problems will find solutions and that God has some tremendous fellow-workers, some outstanding partners out there."

How we think together about violence matters. In our culture, it's tempting to delegate critical thinking about violence entirely to psychologists, criminologists, social workers, or anyone else who deals with violent people. But it doesn't take expertise to do harm, be harmed, or care about people harming each other. The appeal to authority becomes a fallacy here if we expect authority to not merely inform us about violence but also shield us from coping with our community's violence. For example, some communities provide settings in which the victim and offender can face each other to deal with a crime. This is often called "restorative justice." You may know of the story of Paul Rusesabagina from the film *Hotel Rwanda*. Rusesabagina turned a Belgian luxury hotel which he managed into a safe refuge during the genocidal slaughter in Rwanda during 1994, using his courage and cleverness to save over a thousand lives. He speaks of the old system of community justice in Rwanda which needed to be revived. It was a restorative approach to dealing with conflicts. Read through his account and imagine how this would work in the United States. By the way, it is already being used in many American juvenile court systems and elsewhere:

> "Perhaps this simple act taps into something in our national memory. Banana beer is known as 'the drink of reconciliation.' It plays an important role in our traditional local court system, known in the Kinyarwandan language as *gacaca*, or as it is loosely translated, "justice on the grass." If somebody had a problem with a neighbor he would not seek revenge. He instead brought it to the attention of a group of men who we called elders. They were not elected in the classical sense of ballots, but they were put in a position of leadership by a kind of unspoken common assent. To be an elder, you had to have a reputation for fairness and sober judgment, something that would only become apparent over time. It was apparent in the way you lived your life. Hardliners and loud-mouths did not get to be elders.

> "The elders would invite the village to come sit under the shade of a tree and hear the opposing sides tell their stories. Almost all of the disputes concerned property. A stolen goat, for instance, or somebody trying to grow

crops on a hill that belonged to another family. More serious cases—such as those involving violence—were always referred to the courts, but village elders were given wide latitude to help solve local problems.

"After the two enemies had finished speaking, the elders would give their opinions, one by one, on what should be done to remedy the problem. It usually involved compensation. A typical punishment for a stolen goat would be to repay the man a goat—and then give him another as a fine. Somebody bringing a charge thought to be false would be ordered to pay the man he had slandered. Confession was always the key. The village put a high value on the act of admitting culpability, even if you were the one bringing the case. It was viewed as a necessary step in the process of absolution. A man who lied before the entire village knew that he would have to wear that lie for years to come. There was an enormous incentive to come clean, and very little penalty was meted out for being honest with the public, and with yourself.

"Then came the most important part of justice on the grass: the two aggrieved men were required to share a gourd of banana beer as a sign of renewed friendship. There were usually no lasting scars because it was hard to stay angry at someone who had humbled himself before you. The adversarial system of justice practiced in the West often fails to satisfy us, I am convinced, because it does not offer warring parties the opportunity to be human with each other at the end. Whether you were the victim or the aggressor you had to strip yourself of pride and recognize the basic humanity of the fellow with whom you were now sharing a banana beer. There was public shame in this system, true, but also a display of mutual respect that closed the circle. Everyone who showed up to hear the case was invited to sip the banana beer too, as a symbol of the accused man's reconciliation with the entire people. It was like a secular communion. The lasting message for all that gathered there was that solutions could always be found inside—inside communities and inside people." —*An Ordinary Man* by Paul Rusesabagina (Viking: 2006), pp. 8–10

"A breathless first-grader runs up to the school administrator supervising the playground. 'Mrs. Tciu! Mrs. Tciu!' he exclaims. 'I need a talking piece!' Mrs. Ticiu reaches into her pocket, extracts a small plastic dinosaur, and offers it to the child. He grasps the dinosaur tightly in his fist and dashes off to join several other students who, moments earlier, were arguing. With the help of the talking piece, they discuss their disagreement and find a solution they all like." — *The Little Book of Circle Processes* by Kay Pranis (2005)

Share No. 22 A "peace circle" is a format for community of discourse which has its roots in many tribal cultures, including American indigenous and First Nations tribes. Those with a conflict gather in a circle with family, friends, and a circle-keeper who opens and closes the discussion with ceremony. The opening ceremony affirms the values the participants share. The closing ceremony summarizes what the circle has accomplished. A "talking piece" is passed around the circle. A participant may speak only while holding the talking piece. No one may interrupt. When you receive the talking piece, you may speak, pause in silence, or simply pass it to the next person. All members have agreed to speak honestly, with respect, compassion, and with confidentiality. Each person tells a story about the topic at hand, sharing from their experience. They end by reaching consensus on a decision or else simply talk about their experience with an issue to gain mutual understanding. You can imagine children learning to handle a school discipline issue this way. Think of a conflict which hurts you or people you know and arrange for the participants to talk in such a circle. Remember that it has no leaders. All speakers are equals. Report on the results. Note: Start with a low-key misunderstanding or conflict. However, if participants want to apologize or grant forgiveness to each other, allow for that. Emotional and spiritual honesty matter here. It's not a classroom exercise or a game. It's work to resolve real conflicts that arise in thinking together. Write up the results in a three-page essay. Did the format of the circle facilitate any progress in resolving the conflict?

Let's think about a new skill for ethical practice which can help us deal with conflicts that worthwhile critical thinking creates. Call it the skill of *sufficiency*. Knowledge may be an ongoing and never-ending journey which is longer and broader than any individual's agenda or a community's needs. That's one metaphor. However, within a community, a discourse reaches a point where their collaboration is completed. This completion may be marked by a group decision, or by force of logic, or by the topic becoming moot or no longer substantial. Scholarship on this topic is no longer productive. This is when creative thinkers urge us to "think outside the box" but this is a crate which the community has worked hard to assemble. When it is finally assembled, it is not a lack of imagination to say "finished." The topic's time has simply run out, at least for this group. In a sense, the peace circle is an application of this skill in which the discussion comes "full circle" to the point of completion, marked by ceremony and consensus.

When sufficiency has been acknowledged, the work may belong to other communities. In the best possible non-tautological sense, enough is enough for the matter at hand. It is a discipline to practice "enough," because the temptation exists to be satisfied with less or to keep pushing a topic beyond the group's ability to think critically about it simply because the topic has a high priority. The community might also identify itself so strongly with the topic at hand, that it has not yet learned how to shift gears and remain a community of discourse. When nothing in critical thinking persists except persistence, then critical thinking becomes pointless. Just as curiosity begins critical thinking and objectivity lets it mature, sufficiency permits the group to harvest.

We have a strong need for this ethical skill. It's not being resigned to mediocrity, comfort, or lack of progress. Neither is it exhaustion or refusal to be open-minded. Even philosophers who insist that there are no final answers will concede that, when you discover that you've answered a question as well as the question requires, it's time for a new question.

I hope that you start, join, or sustain a community of discourse in which critical thinking thrives enough so that there's plenty to share. Don't say "good-bye" or "the end" if the question is left begging. After all, that is a fallacy.

The Latin and French root of "charity" (caritas) means love, though in our culture charity has come to mean something quite different. Often "charity" means providing unilateral assistance to someone who can't afford it and maybe doesn't deserve it. People who think this way about "charity" believe that accepting charity turns you into an object of pity. Charity is thus incompatible with respecting a person's humanity. That's a long way from love! What's missing in our devolved sense of charity is any sense of interdependence, good will, or empathy with the needs of others. Each of us needs charity sooner or later. And we also need to give it. That applies not just to money, food, and clothing, but to our reasoning as well. The principle of charity is not a handout to the argumentatively challenged. It's a covenant in a community of discourse to provide respect and comprehension which each of us needs.

Share No. 23 Come up with a name for a new non-profit organization devoted exclusively to the charity of mending broken arguments and healing sickly reasoning. This is not a new school. Schools, like hospitals, wait for the needy to find them. Your agency provides the true paramedics of the intellect who move out as a rapid reaction force to sustain struggling thinkers who are in critical condition or at risk. You have just been awarded a grant of $1,000,000 to pursue this work. Where would you start and who would you put on the Board of Directors? Make up an application that someone would need to fill out to qualify for your organization's assistance. After all, you don't want to waste your resources on people who belong in a school or could very well help themselves, do you? Specify who does not qualify and be clear about your criteria for eligibility. There's plenty of stupidity, bad reasoning, and bias in the world, so you'll have to know how to target your efforts carefully to be effective. Finally, become the first applicant. Unless you are convinced that you stand in no need whatsoever of improvement, assistance, or rescue in your attempts to make sense of things, make the best possible case for why you are an ideal candidate for the organization's assistance.

Remember that photo of me on a yacht at the beginning of the book? Clyde Zuber took the picture and actually cropped it from its original size. He chose the somewhat heroic upward angle and also chose to exclude any other persons on board the yacht and all the other boats around the yacht. One picture is truly worth a thousand unfounded inferences. Because we are surrounded by electronic images, we tend to rely upon them for our cues about what is *substantial* and worth our attention. We spontaneously make inferences and draw conclusions from the images we receive. But you can't step outside the frame of those pictures to check your facts, can you? What seems to matter to us could just be a reaction to all those images. That's not the same thing as figuring out what you and your community really need in your time together. You need to figure that out because, although a picture lasts forever, you don't, and neither does the world outside the picture frame.

Share No. 24 This present is one you can share with a three-person group. Have each person bring home movies, scrapbooks, or other collections of photos that include that person or their family. Don't try to explain what the photos are about. Don't answer questions about them. You can include a personal letter or an e-mail that you're comfortable about sharing. Just make them available to each other. Next, have each person write a 3 page essay describing the life and background of the other two group members, based upon the visual evidence. Each person then gets to review the others' essays and decide how accurate they are. What did they misunderstand or leave out? Write your own 3 page essay explaining the inaccuracies and false assumptions. Also, give your partners credit for making good inferences based upon the information available. How did they reach those conclusions?

> "Few human activities convey the allure and the dangers of secrecy as vividly as do the secret societies that have sprung up in so many parts of the world. From primitive times to our own, these secret groups have served the desires for intimacy, enjoyment, knowledge, and power ... Few experiences of secrecy are more intense, or give insiders so stark a sense of separation from outsiders." — *Secrets: On The Ethics of Concealment and Revelation* (1983) by Sissela Bok

Applying the principle of scholarship won't succeed if we're naïve about the accessibility of the facts we need. Some facts are unavailable only because no one has bothered to find them out. Other facts are deliberately concealed. When keeping certain facts secret secures power or profit for the secret-keeper, don't expect to find your answers through an Internet search engine. Fraternities and sororities often have secret rituals or information that only members know. It helps to forge solidarity, though at the expense of a wider community. In high school, these groups are called "cliques." Greek organizations at their best try to compensate for the secrecy by emphasizing their service to the wider community. Secrets protect privacy and security, forge loyalties, but hidden information also keeps communities of discourse from reasoning with confidence.

If secrecy is so important, is curiosity ethical? You may recall the skill of curiosity as being important to applying the Principle of Scholarship. "Curiosity" doesn't usually make the cut for philosophers' lists of moral virtues. Nor do any try to argue that it's an absolute moral duty (what German philosopher Immanuel Kant termed a "categorical imperative.") Philosophers such as Jeremy Bentham and John Stuart Mill argued for a "utilitarian" ethics in which actions are good if they serve the greatest good for the greatest number of people, but you might not want to make such a sweeping claim for curiosity.

In fact, it's not easy to think of many encouraging or inspiring clichés or platitudes about curiosity. Poking around, snooping, and asking questions aren't universally admired, and probably not by the person who's the target of curiosity. Even when we concede that curiosity might be normative and certainly useful for a detective, journalist, or scientist, we seem to suspect or discourage it elsewhere. Curiosity appears unseemly and unsettling, particularly to a community that is a bit intellectually lazy or uncomfortable with disclosure. However, a community of discourse which takes the principle of scholarship seriously needs curiosity desperately. Otherwise, members of that community wind up talking to themselves about things they already know (or think they know), unnourished by investigation.

Share No. 25 Simply counting accurately ought to be the simplest form of scholarship. We need that kind of patient curiosity to make informed judgments. However, counting certain things can be difficult and politically contentious. This share is one you might not want to accept. It requires a "body count." Do a casualty report about the U.S. war in Iraq. Find out how many people died as a result of the regime of Saddam Hussein, and how that occurred. Next, find out how many U.S. soldiers have been killed, how many have been wounded, and how many suffer post-traumatic stress syndrome. Finally, get a count of the number of Iraqis who have died during the Gulf War (Operation Desert Storm) and the war in Iraq. Describe the sources for your information. Do you have good reason to accept the figures as accurate? Do you have doubts about their accuracy? Why? Do the numbers lead you to any conclusions, or are they just numbers?

> "In his age of celebrity, Newton was asked how he had discovered the law of universal gravitation. 'By thinking on it continually' was the reply … What he thought on, he thought on continually, which is to say exclusively, or nearly exclusively, …" — *Never At Rest* — *A Biography of Isaac Newton* by Richard S. Westfall (1980)

The principle of scholarship for a sustaining argument is to acknowledge and deal with the obstacles to knowledge effectively enough to investigate the truth of propositions, test the strength of inferences, and evaluate the merits of an argument. However, there are other forms of scholarship. What counts as true scholarship if you are discovering or inventing something? Is it strictly research in a laboratory or perusing ancient manuscripts? According to biographer Richard Westfall, Sir Isaac Newton was a truly persistent thinker and investigator. He was as much single-minded as curious about formulating the laws of celestial motion. Bodybuilder Bob Paris was just as persistent and driven in his quest to become Mr. Universe and to discover whether he could physically accomplish that goal. The subculture of bodybuilding isn't exactly a community of discourse, or is it? Why does Newton's persistent investigation and discovery of nature's laws look more like scholarship to us than does Paris' trial-and-error quest to discover how to build an ultimate physique?

> "A vision — a fantastical, imaginary movie clip — has continually run through my mind during this last year. I am climbing, climbing, all alone, to the top of this enormous mountain. I fall sometimes — a lot, actually, hurt myself, get up, climb some more, fall down again. It seems as if I've been climbing this mountain forever. After a while, when I'm close enough to the top to see it through breaks in the cloud cover, I pull out my map, to see where I am, and discover that I've gone up the wrong mountain…." — *Gorilla Suit* by Bob Paris (1997)

Here are two very persistent people. Though he came to question his own single-minded ambition, Bob Paris did show a fo-cused commitment in order to become Mr. Universe, and he tack-led bodybuilding until he reached that competitive goal and the public glory and fame that went with it. Isaac Newton had the same sort of persistence when he tackled universal gravitation. (Oddly, he didn't share his discovery until years afterwards). We would tend to think of Newton as applying the principle of scholarship, but not Bob Paris.

Share No. 26 This share may take awhile for you to recover a dividend. Is Bob Paris' weight-lifting or books on the subject a form of scholarship or at least research that can be used by oth-ers? He shared the fruits of his labors with an admiring public. Newton apparently kept his discovery to himself for years. Lift-ing iron doesn't look like research, but Paris had to discover through trial and error how to achieve a world-class physique. Write a 4 page essay answering the question. Keep in mind that Paris has written several weight-training books as a result of his training and success. Newton was creatively applying the physics he knew to explain the motion of the moon and an apple by the same principles.

Have you ever seen the famous rendering of the evolution of the horse? There are a series of horses, beginning with the smallest at one end and culminating with the largest at the other. What does the picture tell you about evolution? Write your answer before read-ing Rifkin's account below:

> "About 1905, an exhibit was set up [in the American Museum of Natural History] showing all these horses ... They were arranged in order of size. Everybody inter-preted them as a genealogical series. But they are not a genealogical series; there is no descent among them. They were found at different times, in different places and they're merely arranged according to size. But it's impossible to get them out of the textbooks ... As a matter of fact, many of the biologists themselves forget

what they are... ." — Dr. Norman Macbeth quoted in
Algeny by Jeremy Rifkin (1983)

Share No. 27 Again, we have to watch out for our own unfounded inferences. At the heart of scholarship is not certainty,
but conflict. The principle of conflict tells us that arguing about
matters of substance will predictably lead us into conflicts. Here's
your assignment: Do an Internet search on the subject of "**abiotic oil**." Find out what it is, and what is claimed about abiotic
oil in scientific, economic, and political terms. Some authorities
seem to believe that it exists. Other authorities deny that it exists. What standards would you apply to resolve this conflict?
Write up your findings in a 4 page essay, carefully citing your
sources.

Here's a fictional account of a real conflict in public policy dealing with climate change. Consider it the starting point for your
Share 28:

Deep in the sweltering heat of mall-strewn and theme park-in-
fested Orlando, Florida, Barbara, the cheerful and hopeful director of Moderate Mitigation in Climate Killers of the Everglades
Environment, decides to combine MMICKEE with a different climate activist group led by Ben. Barbara has her doubts about Ben's
Mature Adaptation to Unstoppable Sizzling and Sinking (MAUSS),
and she finds Ben cynical, arrogant, and too closely tied to vested
political and financial interests. Still, she wants to work with him
and sincerely believes that collaboration is the ethical key to success.
All over Florida, Barbara has politely, patiently, but persistently
championed initiatives to reduce carbon emissions. She carries a
state-of-the-art solar panel as her visual aid. Citing Brazil's success,
Barbara promotes ethanol to diminish Florida's use of oil for transportation and heating. Barbara is convinced that such mitigation
measures, however minor and measly each one of them may appear,
can add up to meaningful change. She also wants to build widespread participation by citizens in all economic and social groups
to fight destructive climate change. Barbara loves to quote William

James about embracing a "moral equivalent to war" though she does not like to be called a "militant."

At MAUSS rallies, Ben rolls his eyes, crosses his arms, and mocks MMICKEE's crusade as a worn-out mantra of public asceticism that didn't work for President Carter, and, even if the public complied, wouldn't stop climate change. Inconvenient and costly economic changes are futile. (MAUSS recently received the Good-As-Green Award from Ben's former employers in the Petroleum Progress Alliance.) Smugly, Ben makes the patronizing point that no amount of carbon reduction or fuel substitutes will refreeze the polar water melting from Greenland's ice sheet each year and which will raise sea level 5 inches within 25 years, and 20 inches by the year 2100. Gazing towards Miami, Ben says that his audience may as well enjoy beaches now, because they will sink with their hotels and condos like an overpriced concrete Atlantis. Ben warms to his Jerimiah role, and he declares that we must grow up and adapt to problems that can't be fixed: the Everglades is doomed, droughts will increase, hurricanes will become more frequent and intense, and wildfires will rage. He can't resist taking one more dig at MMICKEE and suggests they find ways to keep society intact when the angry public realizes that carbon piety hasn't halted climate change.[4]

---

4. Promoting adaptation is not necessarily reactionary. On this view, mitigation might prevent the worst climate scenarios, but we remain responsible for helping the most vulnerable live through unavoidable climate outcomes. If we count upon repentance alone to save us, the road to hell might be paved with carbon credits. A closely related concept is "resilience." "Resilience is the capacity of a system to absorb disturbances and still retain its basic function and structure.... Our resource base, planet Earth, is shrinking while our population continues to expand. The response from most quarters has been for 'more of the same' that got us into this situation in the first place: more control, more intensification, and greater efficiency ... Life is full of surprises.

Sometimes we take them in stride; some times they trip us up." — *Resilience Thinking — Sustaining Ecosystems and People in a Changing World* by Brian Walker and David Salt (2006).

Barbara hears about Ben's rants at MAUSS rallies. Though she hasn't given up on working with Ben's group, she fears that his approach undermines MMICKEE's mission by preaching passivity and resignation at a time when urgent collective action is needed. Barbara reasons that it's a simple matter of cause and effect that our industrial lifestyle produced global warming, so changing that lifestyle is the only reasonable environmental priority. At her church-sponsored MMICKEE gathering, she invites people to join her in prayer. Barbara lowers her voice reverently and seeks forgiveness for our sins against Creation. She pledges that she and her followers will make the necessary sacrifices cheerfully and in good faith to receive divine blessing upon their land.

Ben hears about MMICKEE's public prayer, but he refuses to talk about religion, considering it irrelevant to the incontrovertible scientific facts of the situation. Ben objects that MMICKEE's mitigation crusade is wishful Quixotic thinking which will fool people into thinking that nothing bad will happen if they make enough sacrifices. Ben declares that if one thinks critically and with integrity, one must face the facts and adjust to them instead of moralizing about them.

Share No. 28 According to the Principle of Conflict, we should expect substantial issues to create conflicts for a community of discourse to work through. Make up your own climate activism group which is scientifically credible, morally responsible, and politically astute. Describe your group's vision and mission. Could your group resolve the conflict between your contentious allies, MMICKEE and MAUSS? If not, should they disband and join your group? Identify the sorts of conflicts on this issue. By the way, the cheap MMICKEE MAUSS joke doesn't mean that Walt Disney World and the Disney Corporation have not undertaken worthwhile environmental initiatives. Research its Nature Preserve in Florida. Compare its environmental record to that of other large-scale entertainment theme parks. That would be fair and informative. Just don't forget that, however we wind up treating nature, it's not a theme park for our entertainment.

Chapter Three

Thinking of Fallacies as
Ethical Issues

In critical thinking, you learn to recognize and avoid fallacies. Technically, a fallacy is a misconception resulting from incorrect reasoning and is often called a "counterfeit argument" because a fallacy appears to be a valid and sound argument though it is not.

However, is committing a fallacy *wrong* in a moral or ethical sense? Should we apologize for or even repent of our fallacies, or just regard them as errors in reasoning that need to be corrected? We could excuse ourselves by declaring that arguments commit fallacies. People don't commit fallacies. That's technically true. Still, we can look for blame in both the person who commits the fallacy and the person who accepts it. Even a person who commits (or makes an argument which commits) a fallacy in good faith has still done something that can undermine her thinking. A person who fails to spot a fallacy will still suffer consequences of credulity and gullibility.[1]

---

1. To the best of my knowledge, not much research or attention is given to the ethical topography of familiar fallacies. Exposing and citing fallacies does seem to give authors of critical thinking texts a much-needed license to show humor, cultural relevance, shock, disdain, and loyalty to standards. Still, even when purveyors of *ad hominem* are scolded, crafty salesmen are chided, and shameless politicians are exposed to (the author's) contempt, the blame-finding does not explore the varieties of ethical relationships which we enter into by making or acting upon one sort of fallacy or another. In the spirit of exploring the ethical practice of crit-

In other words, fallacies can be committed innocently, but many are crafted and carried out as deliberate attempts to persuade in ways that circumvent or undermine successful argumentation. Either way, fallacies often have moral consequences. Fallacies aren't just bad reasoning inside someone's head. They are ultimately antisocial and raise ethical as well as logical issues. Rather than try to think about the ethics of fallacies in general, let's look at some specific examples.

A. Appeal to Authority

During my sophomore year in college, I decided to try sport parachuting. I did some research and discovered a club on campus authorized by the University. I talked to its student leaders who could claim to have made hundreds of jumps safely. The President of the club (a senior) also appeared very helpful and sensible. The other members of the club vouched for him too. On this basis, I let him pack my chute and direct me out of a Cessna at 3,000 feet, confident that he knew what he was doing and that I could trust his judgment. I did not investigate the club's history or past accidents. I knew nothing about anyone's licenses, certification, or training. I had no real idea of the risk involved. Still, I thought I was making a rational albeit edgy choice.

Inexplicably, my parents did not think that I had good reason to appeal to this club's president as an authority to justify my skydiving adventure. They suggested that my new-found authority (a.k.a. "some stupid kid") was no one I should be trusting with my life. Suspicious that my parents would reject any student authority, I patiently and patronizingly invoked the august authority of the university itself which had deemed this club worthy of student ac-

---

ical thinking, I do so in this chapter. I hope this tentative "share" begins a continuing scholarly conversation on this topic.

tivity funds, and had therefore sanctioned its activities. That didn't work. I then used the authority of empirical evidence: none of the club's members had suffered so much as a scratch from skydiving (or if they had, they weren't talking to me about it). I decided to keep skydiving. I also decided that parental authority is pretty jealous of any competition.

Welcome to the "appeal to authority." Many critical thinking textbooks view "the appeal to authority" as a fallacy involving reliance upon mere testimony rather than original facts. A claim is not true just because someone authoritative claims it to be true. Other texts speak of the "appeal to *questionable* authority" and view the fallacy as one of attributing authority inappropriately to someone who is not an expert in the matter at hand. Both situations could compromise an argument, but this caution against appealing to authorities must be confusing to first year students who are told to carefully cite all the authorities they quote. This prompts a reasonable question: When should you rely on your own judgment or trust the judgment of someone who has the reputation of an expert? The fact that much of your education amounts to learning from and trusting the testimony of authorities makes it difficult to say when we are committing the fallacy of appeal to authority.

It could be a false dilemma. Believing everything you're told or believing nothing you're told are both unrealistic all-or-nothing reactions to authority. At times, "believing nothing" really means a private resolve to become so self-sufficient that you don't have to rely upon any authority. But you can't realistically be self-sufficient to the point of having first-hand acquaintance with the facts at stake in every argument that you care about. We have to accept that we rely upon authority most of the time. We can try to be good judges of appropriate authority, but ultimately it's still a matter of learning how and when to extend informed and appropriate trust. The ethical issue is one of how we justify that trust as a relationship with an authority. A community of discourse not only sustains good arguments but also works out credible standards to guide and inform our trust with respect to authorities for the area of expertise in question.

Trust does carry risk, but not necessarily unlimited risk. Trust doesn't have to be blind, unqualified or unjustified. Trust doesn't imply that we regard an authority on one subject as utterly trustworthy for all purposes. It does mean that we extend *trust according to the needs and standards of the community's ongoing discourse.* That is a truly ethical enterprise, involving choice about our relationships with those in whom we have placed our trust, as well as loyalty to standards for offering trust to an appropriate extent and with respect to appropriate expertise. None of this removes the element of risk inherent in trust. Rather, we make choices about where we are willing to take risks. Whether we try to go it alone, work within a community, or trust others, there is no entirely risk-free road to knowledge.

Who counts as a trustworthy authority? I once considered hiring a man to landscape my yard because I had discussed gardening with him for several years and was impressed by the range and depth of his knowledge of botany and landscape design. I could tell from his work at other sites that he spoke with demonstrated authority when he described how different trees, plantings, and flowers of different sorts would provide seasonal color and variety all year long.

As he surveyed my yard, I was ready to give him the job when I noticed a nasty scar on his forearm. When I inquired about it, he replied matter-of-factly that he had received it during his abduction by the "grays." At this point, I was too stunned to regard him as an expert or authority about anything at all. I could only see him as a crazy person babbling about flying saucers. Certainly, I thought, he must be crazy since only crazy people talk about such things (Do you recognize arguing in a circle?). And yet he hadn't lost any expertise about plants and could be trusted to tell the difference between annual and perennial plantings. For all I know, he could be trusted to recognize "grays" when he saw them too, but I do know that I've never seen any aliens and would rather not believe that they exist. I'm not sure whom I would trust to be an authority on that subject. What would your standards be? I expect that support groups for self-identified alien abductees are just as concerned about authority. Who is crazy ? Who is lying? Who is trying to tell the truth? And who might make a good landscaper?

Share No. 29 You are thinking about massive and intimidating world problems such as war, poverty, injustice, and ecological destruction. Where would you look for authoritative "ghost busters" to help you solve or at least better understand these global problems? Who, if anyone, counts as an authority with the requisite knowledge, experience, and credentials? You might rely upon a political leader or diplomat who participates in making peace between warring parties. To handle ecological destruction, you could consult the Union of Concerned Scientists since they seem to have the appropriate mission and technical competence. But these are multi-disciplinary or perhaps trans-disciplinary problems which are political, scientific, spiritual, economic, ethical, and legal problems all rolled together. That makes it even more of a challenge to find appropriate authority and expertise. You don't want expertise at the cost of sacrificing your best judgment to another's opinions, but you want to learn from someone likely to teach and guide in a way you can legitimately respect.

Go ask your grandmothers. Read about the International Council of the Thirteen Indigenous Grandmothers. There are a variety of references online, including their current website at www.grandmotherscouncil.com.

Next, describe the types of authority they possess for the world with respect to the global problems which matter to you. Elderly women or "old ladies" may not be people you're accustomed to regard seriously as authorities, but keep an open mind as you research them. Finally, e-mail or mail a question to one of grandmothers about which you expect that woman to have some trustworthy credibility. If these leaders are not available to you, start talking with the grandmothers whom you know or need to know, and find out their particular authority and expertise. What is your question which deals with a substantial issue and appropriately makes use of the sort of authority which the grandmother possesses? In a four-page essay, describe your question, the response, and the type of authority which is appropriate to the relationship you've entered into with this share.

B. Begging the Question

Begging the question is committed when our argument assumes the truth of the very matter in question. In essence, the argument's conclusion is already contained in the premises. The conclusion simply restates something of the premises in different words. This is also called "arguing in a circle." Because textbooks tend to give examples that are as obvious as possible to illustrate the fallacy clearly ("How long have you been beating your wife?" or "God exists because the Bible says so, and the Bible is true because God wrote it."), you might have the impression that it's all about trivial and transparent tautologies that couldn't fool any intelligent person. But if you argue in a big enough circle or with sufficient subtlety, you can sound profound rather than repetitious.

The funniest version of begging the question I've encountered was delivered by a female student in class when a computer science classmate informed her that much of the Internet "information highway" consists of pornography sites. Genuinely shocked and outraged, she spun around in her chair to glare at the guys who happened to be sitting in the back of the room and loudly demanded "*Is that true?*" I'll let you imagine the expressions on their faces.

Actually, it's the activity of intelligence that often sets us up for this fallacy. Begging the question often happens as we attempt to think further about our propositions by reformulating them in other words. It's a natural tactic by which we try to get a fresh perspective on our own ideas. But we can wind up tricking ourselves (and others) if we're not careful, by thinking that we're not just rephrasing, but actually making an argument, reasoning from one clear and distinct proposition to another separate and distinct proposition.

In fact, when we beg the question, it seems that we've come up with quite a brilliant argument because the truth of it is seemingly irrefutable. It's even more convincing when this happens in a group. When a dozen people of like mind start to express and endorse one and the same idea in their own words and out of their own experience, it sounds as though they're coming up with a wealth of reasons for agreeing with the idea or even collectively forming an argument for the idea. So, what began as a tropical storm of useful variations grows to a Category 4 hurricane of massive but ultimately circular proportions.

Loyalty can also create a pretext for begging the question. We want to preclude or preempt any objection to a matter which seems obviously true and which is important to us. Think of begging the question as a misguided attempt to be loyal to some truth that we cherish by dressing it up in a premature argument. When someone begs the question, they are trying to preclude further argument by presenting something as too obviously true to allow for disputation. Yes, an argument which amounts to "If A, then A," is irrefutable, but it is also not much of an argument. Suppose you ask why I trust my friend, and I reply that she is so worthy of confidence and devotion that I find her genuinely trustworthy. You accuse me of begging the question because "worthy of confidence and devotion" means virtually the same thing as "trustworthy." You declare that I'm saying that my friend is trustworthy because she is trustworthy.

Does that mean my friend isn't trustworthy? No. Does it mean that it's irrational for me to trust my friend? No. It means that I haven't given you reasons yet as to why I should trust her. I haven't yet argued with sufficient care and honesty to expose, test, and confirm my assumptions about my friend for your benefit. Maybe I can't justify my intuitions about my friend's trustworthiness well enough to offer an argument, even if my intuitions are accurate.

Though begging the question is sometimes referred to as "arguing in a circle," it's a circle in more than one sense. Ethical issues crop up in this fallacy either because we've let our vortex of variations become a circular storm, or because a loyalty creates a "circle" with the arguer on the inside and the rest of the community of discourse on the outside. This inside/outside division keeps the community of discourse from functioning as a community.

Share No. 30 A practical place to wrestle with begging the question is pulling yourself up by your own bootstraps. It's been centuries since we actually grabbed real bootstraps to hoist ourselves upright, but we know about things which can start themselves, as when a computer "boots." Some prophecies are self-fulfilling. Suppose you need to "boot" an argument for making a certain New Year's resolution. Pick a resolution which matters to you. The conclusion to your argument would be that you will therefore honor the resolution. Make a careful inventory of how and why you failed to honor past resolutions on this topic. List credible reasons why you will honor the resolution on this occasion. Compare these reasons against any contrary indications. Now, describe the assistance or circumstances which would make it most likely that you'll keep the resolution. Here's the hard part: You are *not* allowed to deprecate or insult yourself as part of your reasons for predicting failure. That's not a reason. It's begging the question. You are *not* allowed to cite your innate perseverance or desperation as evidence in favor of predicting that you will honor the resolution. That's begging the question. It doesn't matter whether you are *trying* to prove that you will honor the pledge to yourself. It matters whether, in fact, you reason well for that conclusion. Show your written argument anonymously to someone with good judgment and ask whether they'd reach the conclusion that you would honor the resolution and not just beg the question. Good luck!

C. Appeals to Emotion

Critical thinking texts especially condemn fallacious arguments which persuade without convincing, stating that such arguments use emotions in the place of reasons to support a conclusion. We also appeal to emotions in order to manipulate others. However, that doesn't mean that the ethics of argumentation requires us to quash all feelings and all reference to feelings in order to argue well. Nor does it mean every attempt to make an emotional connection with others in our arguments must be rejected as manipulative or as mere rhetoric. As we consider this group of fallacies (including appeals to pity, rage, humor, fear, envy, and hatred) from the standpoint of ethical argumentation, we need to decide when our arguments incorporate emotions wrongly and when it might be justifiable to acknowledge emotions in our arguments and arguing.

For example, It is not automatically a *faux pas* in logic to acknowledge the emotional significance of the issue at hand, nor is it a fallacy to argue in ways that acknowledge and honor the full weight of the loyalties, resources, attachments, aversions, and assumptions of a community of discourse. Good reasoning, as a matter of course, shouldn't automatically exclude all consideration of motives and feelings. What we want to avoid is tricking people into agreeing with a proposition by playing upon their feelings. The emotional solidarity of a community matters, but we don't want to purchase it at the price of ceasing to be a genuine community of discourse.

Advertisers and politicians are the usual suspects for tricky dealing in critical thinking textbooks. If you see an ad or campaign speech cited, it won't be as role models of ethical argumentation. In the interest of fair play, perhaps we should not assume that we already know why they are effective and pervasive. Do they truly have sorcerer-like power to transform us from citizens into pig-like consumers simply by appealing to our feelings? If so, then perhaps the problem is not manipulation but the fact that our feelings have been sorely neglected.

That is, perhaps advertising and political rhetoric are culturally powerful not because they deploy diabolically seductive fallacies, but because they target people's needs and wants. Our typical version of rational discourse has burdened itself with an ascetic disdain for emotions, and such discourse consequently has difficulty using reason in ways that address people's needs and wants. Being rational shouldn't mean abstaining from recognizing how people feel and what they truly want and need. Advertisers and politicians might really be ignoring deeper spiritual and human needs that people have, but that's another issue. Perhaps those wants and needs (like the need for a community of discourse) can't be satisfied by consuming.

At any rate, if people's needs and wants and living circumstances are not addressed appropriately by rational discourse, and, if people's real motives are treated as if they don't really matter (or shouldn't matter for the sake of argument), then we shouldn't blame fallacies for the lack of good arguments in our culture. This is one reason for emphasizing *the principle of substance* in making a sustaining argument. What we condemn as pandering to subjectivity may be perceived as a much-needed acknowledgment of and respect for our subjective life of feelings and motives. Arguers can and should be emotional, in whatever style their personality dictates, to successfully communicate their feeling about their arguments and deal with the reality and relevance of emotion to reaching conclusions and making decisions, without, for that reason, being any less sound in their reasoning. They choose to take responsibility for their emotions.

In fact, a successful argument as defined here implies that those engaged in the arguing do, in fact, care about what they discuss and that they communicate with each other effectively. Hiding ones feelings is not the same as being more rational. Just as cooperation and competition (when guided by mutual respect, logical strength, and a commitment to arguing about what matters) can both yield sustaining arguments, so too we can have a sustaining argument regardless of whether the disputants are mild-mannered and deferential or volatile, noisy, and contentious. If we're concerned about not introducing biases or pandering to feelings in our arguments, the solution is not to anesthetize our discourse but to recognize what and how people feel about issues as we attempt to reason together as a community of discourse. We can recognize, express, share, and honor feelings without pandering to or exploiting them.

Hasn't anyone helped this dog yet? Here is a package-deal on appeal to pity and arguing in a circle: "Unless you lovingly adopt this helpless underfed puppy into your home, it won't receive the affection and shelter it so desperately needs and which your compassionate home can provide."

Share No. 31 Appeals to emotion typically target emotions of longing, lack, or lust. These appeals exploit uncomfortable feelings driven by unmet needs and wants. But what if someone appeals to your spontaneous gratitude? Are you grateful simply for being alive to experience one more day of your life? You can feel truly thankful and appreciative even without any specific beliefs about whom or what you should thank. You may delight in nature or appreciate an anonymous gift. You could feel thankful before you know whom to thank or whether there's anyone to thank. What's a fallacious way of appealing to this positive emotion? Imagine that you were in an auto accident which killed everyone involved, except you. Make up the details of the disaster yourself. Decide whether you're to blame for the accident and to what extent. Next, imagine that you feel strong survivor guilt about being the only person in that collision who is still alive. You don't feel worthy of escaping what befell the others, particularly if you're at all to blame for their deaths. You can't manage to reason your way out of this abiding and debilitating emotion. A friend decides not to convince you that your thinking about the past event is faulty. Instead, she advises you to be grateful for simply being alive. Is this direct appeal to emotion a manipulative fallacy or is it consistent with good reasoning about how deal with the aftermath of the accident? Give your best argument!

D. *Ad Hominem*

Ad Hominem is the fallacy of attacking the speaker as a ploy to discredit the speaker's argument. Whether it includes abuse, ridicule, or reference to circumstances, it's not hard to find examples, especially in an election campaign. Critical thinking texts usually describe this ploy of rejecting an argument by attacking the speaker as the exploitation of a hearer's psychological foibles to obscure clear thinking about the issues. Presumably, attacking the speaker muddies the waters so much that we can't distinguish between our feelings about the speaker and the merits of what the speaker argues. When the fallacy of *ad hominem* is committed, someone is using our own psychological biases against us in order to undermine our ability to reason about an argument. *Ad hominem* isn't usually discussed as an ethical issue except to note that it's not nice to play upon prejudice and hatred just to win an argument. Since we really do have strong feelings about certain speakers, what should critical thinkers do about that? Should we ignore those feelings or pretend that they don't exist—literally—for the sake of argument? What is our responsibility for ethical argumentation?

A more honest approach to *ad hominem* and the possibility that good arguments happen to bad people might begin with the admission that our tendency to link bad people with bad arguments isn't completely irrational. Is it so unreasonable to inductively reason that people we dislike and have reason to suspect or condemn may not be expected to offer the most trustworthy discourse for our benefit? Our particular biases may not be as much of a problem as our fixation upon the speaker at the expense of the argument. The key then is to break that fixation for the sake of the argument. Perhaps we can constructively reframe our response to this problem of ad hominem.

For example, instead of having members of a community of discourse pretend to be blind to the moral deficiencies of the speaker or their own biases, they could instead resolve to take personal ownership of the argument for the sake of a community of discourse. That is, the community becomes a "foster home" for the scoundrel's argument as the agreed-upon shared property of the community of discourse, thereby breaking the scoundrel's moral monopoly over (and link with) the argument. In this way, we avoid *ad hominem,* not by being oblivious to the speaker's faults or tiptoeing around our own biases, but by assuming an appropriate ethical responsibility with respect to the speaker and our chosen community of discourse. The argument is not just the personal possession of the scoundrel who is prone to bad arguments. It is a public resource of a community that needs to take ownership and responsibility for the argument, regardless of its source.

For example, as a college student, I read B.F. Skinner's book, *Beyond Freedom and Dignity.* I should say that I began to read the book. Half-way through, I swung the book back over my head and then pitched it violently across the room so that it struck the wall and fell to the floor of my dorm room where it remained, gathering dust for several weeks.

I didn't know what to make of his arguments against free will and human choice. I only knew that I hated what he had to say, considered him a thoroughly despicable person, and regarded his book as too vile to retrieve from the floor. (If you're lucky you encounter at least one author in your college experience who elicits this reaction). I couldn't bring myself to read *Walden Two* or anything else he had written because I was sure that he couldn't write anything worth reading. Over the years, my judgment of Prof. Skinner has softened, and my appreciation for his arguments has increased, even though I still disagree with many of his conclusions. What happened? Did I simply calm down or wise up? No—I continued to think about the issues which he provoked me to consider from different angles until I could find a way to assimilate his arguments into the context of a larger discussion about freedom and responsibility. In short, by continuing to think and learn about the issues, I broke the fixation and rescued the arguments. That defused my *ad hominem* reaction better than trying to pretend that the writer and his ideas did not anger me.

The fallacy concerns various ways in which emotions are exploited. If a community of discourse finds effective ways to acknowledge and honor and express motives, feelings, and desires in the course of arguments, then our subjective life should be less vulnerable to exploitation.

Share No. 32 You may have heard appeals and arguments for helping endangered species, such as gorillas. Advocates for animals are portrayed as courageous crusaders or as sentimental cranks that care more about animals than people. But both crusaders and cranks can share good arguments with us. The trick to avoiding *ad hominem* is not to hide behind a veil of ignorance about the eccentricities of the source, but to instead join a community of discourse about the source's argument, regardless of whether the source has a seat at the community's table. Read the world-famous African ambassador's argument to the Japanese for helping the Gorilla Foundation as set forth at http://www.koko.org/news/Press_Releases/pr_050728_CWSE.html. Here is the text of the article:

> "Aichi, Japan—July 28, 2005. Koko, the world's only talking gorilla, is using her established celebrity status to send a compelling message to Japan where a new gen-

eration of world leaders and politicians are being urged to help save her relatives from extinction. Wildlife conservationist, Aleisha Caruso, will convey Koko's message through an interactive multimedia workshop entitled "Meet Koko — Ambassador for Endangered Species" at the Children's World Summit for the Environment in Aichi, Japan on July 28, 2005.

"Koko the gorilla first made world headlines about 25 years ago when she mastered human sign language and launched a new career — as the ambassador for endangered animals everywhere. This two-hour multimedia workshop will give the children attending the Summit an opportunity to learn about the plight of gorillas and great apes directly through Koko (and her late companion signing gorilla, Michael) as well as to learn some of Koko's language — American Sign Language (ASL) — to help overcome international language barriers in appealing for the world to help save the species.

"The 34-year-old primate — who has a vocabulary of over 1,000 signs (in American Sign Language), understands over 2000 words of spoken English and has appeared on the Internet where she wowed more than 20,000 website visitors with her thoughts on life, love and dreams — has her own ambassadorial message for the Children's World Summit for the Environment in Japan.

"People need to hurry," instructs Koko in her message to more than 1000 schoolchildren attending the summit in Aichi to discuss their concerns on environmental issues and the future of their planet. Addressing children from 150 countries, Koko is the perfect advocate for endangered species — highlighting the need for urgent action to preserve a fragile eco-system where more than 70 species are lost each day.

"We both have the same message," says Ms. Caruso,

the 28-year-old Australian ambassador to the United Nations Great Ape Survival Project (GRASP) who has worked tirelessly giving endangered animals a voice. "We want to make the new generation of world leaders, politicians and compassionate adults aware of the desperate need to protect a species in danger of extinction."

"Schoolchildren joining their Imperial Highnesses Prince and Princess Akishino at the four day event staged by the Japanese Government and the United Nations Environment Program (UNEP) will get a glimpse of some of the endearing characteristics of this gentle primate which Ms. Caruso has witnessed often in her jungle rescue work at sanctuaries and orphanages. Koko—who has enjoyed private meetings with Hollywood actors Robin Williams and Leonardo Di Caprio—will give new insight into the intelligent, gentle personalities of a species now facing extinction.

"Koko and her relatives share 98% of our DNA," explains Ms. Caruso, whose tireless campaign to raise global awareness about the threats facing the great ape population resulted in a powerful new alliance with GRASP as its Australian ambassador. "So this is a fantastic opportunity for everyone to meet her (at least virtually) because she's the only gorilla in the world able to communicate with human beings," she explains.

"Using sign language, Koko will communicate about her life, hopes and dreams which include her desire to have a baby and her love for her pet kitten. "I cannot overemphasize how important it is for us to help Koko have a baby (whether natural or adopted) so that she can teach her offspring sign language and thus ensure that her unique ambassadorship and advocacy for her species is sustained through subsequent generations," adds Ms. Caruso.

"The astonishing gorilla has already addressed more than 20,000 people via the world's only inter-species Internet chats—enthralling fans with her intelligence and revelations that she loves reggae music, romantic movies and video dating. Koko has such a strong sense of identity that she refers to herself as "fine animal person gorilla."

"She's the greatest ambassador for her species," says Ms. Caruso, "because she can speak to us in our own language. She's gentle, loving and smart with an IQ of between 70 and 95. And she's self-aware and funny, even laughing at her own jokes and making up her own words like "eye hat" for "mask."

"But while Koko dances when she's happy and laughs when she's tickled, Koko signed "sad" when her human caregivers discussed the troubles facing her free-living relatives in Africa.

"Tragically, gorillas are just one example of the many animal species under threat of extinction from illegal poaching, devastation of habitat and escalating illegal international trade in wildlife products. In particular, gorillas and other great apes have become innocent victims of the growing illegal "bushmeat" trade, fueled by the human appetite for construction materials and exotic minerals used in cell phones. Now, in an age where fewer than 700 mountain gorillas exist in Africa, and thousands of western lowland gorillas (like Koko and Michael) are being killed each year by bushmeat poachers, it is hoped that Koko will be able to persuade children to help protect endangered animals everywhere.

"Extinction is forever, and it would be tragic to imagine living in a world without fellow sentient beings like Koko," warns Dr. Penny Patterson, President and Director of Research for The Gorilla Foundation, the California-based non-profit that has raised, educated and cared for Koko for over 30 years. "But there's still time, perhaps a decade or two at most, to save gorillas and all of the other great apes from being eliminated by their closest living relatives—humans, if we simply make a conscious effort to show them at least as much kindness as they show us. They have so much to teach us about adapting to nature, communication between species and our role as stewards—not plunderers—of planet Earth."

"Simply raising awareness about conservation facts and principles doesn't seem to work," Dr. Patterson observes, "only empathy for other species can save them—and Koko engenders that empathy. Her role in great ape conservation has become imperative, and we're thrilled that so many future leaders are going to meet her at this world conference. The rest of the world can get acquainted with Koko by visiting www.Koko.org."

Share No. 32 (Continued) Okay, do you take the message or argument of a gorilla talking through sign language seriously? Koko may be a celebrity, but she could still be wrong. If you think so, then you're giving her credit for being either right or wrong on the topic. What is a way of evaluating Koko's advice which does not commit the *ad hominem* fallacy? Yes, we should technically update this fallacy to call it "ad specium" since we might be tempted to dismiss it based on Koko's membership in the class of gorillas.

E. Appeal to Ignorance

Do you notice that both teachers and students seem terribly embarrassed about revealing their own ignorance? That's pretty ironic when you consider what a university is supposed to be about. Embarrassment aside, doesn't ignorance interfere with a community's ability to argue with confidence? What are our ethical responsibilities for arguments when we just don't know enough? The first responsibility is to avoid that classic fallacy *argumentum ad ignoratium*, or the appeal to ignorance. It can take either of two forms. You could argue "There is no evidence proving that a proposition is false, so the proposition must be true." You could also argue, "There is no evidence proving that a proposition is true, so the proposition must be false." It's a fallacy because a lack of evidence for a proposition can't count as evidence either for or against the truth of a proposition. Nonetheless, people who are anxious or embarrassed about their ignorance can find this very appealing.

The appeal to ignorance is also an appeal to our fears and hopes. It's very close to an appeal to emotion: Can you prove without a doubt that the aspirin you're about to swallow *hasn't* been laced with cyanide? Well, can you? Sure, this is about ignorance or at least lack of evidence, but its main appeal is to your *fear*. And we can appeal to hopes too: Can you prove without a doubt that a certain well-known politician *won't* eventually succeed in articulating a complete sentence or come up with a workable idea this time? Sure, he hasn't so far, but that doesn't prove that he never will, right? Ignorance doesn't prove anything, however, one way or another. It just gives breathing space to our hopes and fears. It's not a very ethically responsible way to deal with ignorance.

Forbidden Knowledge: There are a few more complex problems of dealing with ignorance which introduce different ethical issues and which defy easy solutions. Let's say that someone does not have evidence to establish that a proposition is true or false but claims to have good reasons for believing that seeking evidence would be **too dangerous** to undertake on the grounds that some knowledge really deserves to be forbidden because there is good reason to suppose that it would cause serious and irreparable harm. We don't know the evidence yet, but we do have evidence to be justifiably concerned that unearthing *further* evidence would harm ourselves or others. When the evidence sought might unleash some genetic disaster, give tools to a terrorist, or expose the innocent to pornography, the prospect of the volatile and the vile makes us ask about the ethical course of action.

A liberal arts university typically makes a presumption in favor of acquiring evidence and new knowledge. Although it may have rules prohibiting research which violates privacy or consent, if no such violation is at stake, the community is committed to increasing knowledge as a largely unmitigated benefit. Some knowledge may be out of bounds, but no knowledge is intrinsically forbidden or viewed as more dangerous than ignorance. The *appeal to ignorance* objection to research could be called a *defense of society* objection. If society is a fort which needs to be surrounded by a moat filled with ignorance, it's hard to imagine how that moat of deliberate and stubborn ignorance about the matter at hand could sustain any community of discourse about that matter inside the fort.

Share No. 33 You are well-informed about a subject substantial for your community of discourse. There is no serious debate about what you know, though, of course, you don't claim to understand everything about your field. You have consulted the best published authorities on your subject. There is much scholarship required of you because social and political institutions spend much time and resources applying information about this subject. The only people who disagree with your theories are plainly motivated by self-interest, and any honest evaluator would concede this point. That critical minority is far from being disinterested. You do understand that it's nevertheless possible to be hasty and mistaken, so you take care in your community of discourse to discern what is or isn't the case, by any means necessary. You are curious about researching testimony, observing repeated patterns, and resolving conflicts on this subject by consensus and spiritual reflection. However, you have a nagging doubt as a professional that conclusive proof in your field is more difficult than the public supposes. There are still plenty of unanswered questions, and the resulting ignorance leaves you less than certain about the truth of your conclusions at times.

Yes, you are a fifteenth century European scholar of witch-craft. If that sounds a bit too ironic or far-fetched, consider: You want to ensure that the old woman you are about to burn alive is a bona fide witch. You are reasonably certain that she is, since she confessed to witchcraft after intense and excruciating in-terrogation. Her fellow convicted witches corroborated her con-fession. Your colleague objects that the community lacks sufficient information to conclusively prove witchcraft, so she can't be a true witch. How do you counter this evasive appeal to igno-rance? The community can't erase all possible doubt and pre-vent all possible error. That's unrealistic for even the most diligent investigation. You yourself idly speculate that perhaps there re-ally are no witches, but you're responsible for empirical evalu-ation, not metaphysical speculation. Despite the thousands of witches executed during your lifetime, you would not know-ingly persecute an innocent person. The old woman's neighbors told stories about how babies had died in town and crops re-peatedly failed. Of course, no one could personally attest to witnessing her dealings with Satan, but it was well known that no one could be a witch without such dealings. Do you have enough ignorance to deny that she is a witch? How would you remove your ignorance? Write this up in a four-page essay.[2]

Uncorking the Genie in the Lamp. Here is a similar ethical argu-mentation problem created by ignorance. What if new knowledge would be like a genie released from Aladdin's lamp that would for-

---

2. You may decide that knowing about witches or being uncomfortably ignorant about witches begs the question about whether witches really exist. You decide to be an agnostic about this, but will your skepticism save the woman's life in that community of discourse? We may decline to have convictions about the supernatural, but we are accountable for requiring or allowing others to live or die by our assumptions. It's not merely true that a chain of reasoning must start with certain assumptions. The chain also must end with being part of certain ethical relationships and causing certain consequences. We can't shift all the moral credit or blame to our assumptions or lack of them.

ever change the world in ways we could not control and would probably regret? The genie is not demonstrably bad in itself, but its presence in the world might be very bad. We could argue that certain natural or social structures which have prevailed for ages but without rational support, should nevertheless not be tampered with because it is a reasonable presumption that something which has been that durable might also be sufficiently foundational to our lives in ways that exceed our current understanding. Its possible disruption would be likely to create unforeseen and irreparable systemic damage to our lives. The stakes could be too high to risk uncorking the lamp.

The problem is that the corked-up knowledge can't be proven to be bad. We only have a deeply felt hunch that our sustaining structures could be jeopardized. My colleague, Ann Cahill, offered one version of this problem which is really also a variation on begging the question: "X is bad because in twenty years our children will wonder why we ever let X happen." And why will they wonder? Because X was so bad. The argument doesn't prove that X is really bad. However, that doesn't mean that X can't be bad.

You might smell an inconsistency here: How can these sustaining structures of nature and culture be so stable and enduring and simultaneously so fragile and vulnerable that we can't risk testing them? Maybe our own deep reliance upon our cultural traditions and biological interdependence makes us all the more anxious about losing them. Our anxiety might be a bad measure of their true resilience.

Still, environmentalists make such an argument against altering the balance of a given ecosystem. Conservatives arguing against same-sex marriage have also contended that changing the traditional definition of marriage might unleash major consequences commensurate with the major role of traditional marriage in our society. This is not quite the same as worrying about forbidden knowledge which we have some reason to deem dangerous. This is an appeal to the deep order of things which might conceivably be undone by a single small and otherwise unobjectionable bit of knowledge.

This "knowledge genie" is not dangerous if it stays corked in its bottle, but could be hazardous if it's released to invade and alter the deep order of things. Knowledge is irreversible in a sense, because when you come to know something, you can't freely choose to "un-know" it. That might mean that the effects of knowing something may be irreversible too, although that doesn't necessarily follow.

Suppose that certain traditions sustain a community and meet its needs at a more basic level than any particular argument can ever hope to do. If you'll grant that (for the sake of argument?), then consider that the tradition ought to therefore be held exempt from contamination by argument, whether specious or substantial. The risk would far outweigh any potential benefit.

So, we have an appeal to primal caution about changes which have the potential to create a meta-disruption in the sustaining order of things in which we are situated. It's not exactly an appeal to emotion, though fear and hope are involved. It verges upon begging the question without actually committing that fallacy: "We should not learn X because X is dangerous to know ... and it is dangerous precisely because it's one of things we ought not to uncover." This concern for the danger of particular knowledge comes close to making a hypothetical appeal to ignorance: "If we were to know X, then we would be in danger." You might fantasize about what would happen if you knew the future, but biotechnology is no fantasy. If you risked finding out everything about your own genome, would the very possession of that information be something you would avoid seeking?

F. The Appeal to Force
(Argumentum ad Baculum)

Years ago when I and my friend were accosted at night by an armed mugger, my friend told the mugger to "get lost" and proceeded to walk to our car. Our attacker was so stunned and dumbfounded by this lack of cooperation, that he ran after us and repeated his demand for money, waving his gun in our faces. My friend turned and firmly repeated his refusal and then continued to walk away. We drove away unharmed, but I told my friend that his refusal to cooperate was irrational and dangerous. He could have gotten us killed! My friend's response was that cooperating would have been the irrational option. After all, a mugger is not an insurance carrier, and we weren't being offered protection. Simply stated, the mugger could shoot us if we cooperated or shoot us if we refused to cooperate. There's nothing particularly rational about appeasing the mugger.

If this situation leaves you uneasy and conflicted, then you can appreciate why this fallacy is a serious one. The appeal to force tries to turn a threat into an argument and attempts to substitute fear for rational assent. It is compelling only in the sense that physical compulsion is being deployed. The threat has no logical force. It's tempting to fixate on the threat, but, for the person exposed to the threat, the ethical problem isn't how to morally judge the coercion itself, but deciding to take responsibility for reasoning logically and effectively about how to best respond to a particular threat. Cooperation, flight, or resistance are possible reactions, and one could make a good argument for one choice or the other, depending on the circumstances.

What we *can't* do is to resolve the crisis by choosing the "right" conclusion to the aggressor's "argument" because the threat is not an argument, even if it's phrased in "if-then" language or as a choice between alternatives. The real moral issue is whether we have the intellectual integrity to refuse to see the threat as something other than what it is, and the practical ethical skill to discern and choose the best available response to that threat.

Share No. 34 When you untie the ribbons and open this big gift, you're in for a surprise. It's a pre-owned 9mm semi-automatic assault weapon complete with ammunition. In other countries, it's available only to police, but you can own this one, subject, of course, to applicable current state and federal law. I notice that you are startled and speechless about my thoughtful present, so I do my best to reassure you:

"I know that you would use my gift responsibly, and that you'd warn any children in your household not to play with it. The gun would protect you from assault. What could be more ethical? I know that you don't resolve conflicts by appealing to force, and that force itself is no argument. On the other hand, your weapon gives your prospective attacker very good reason not to assault you. What's wrong with providing good reasons when and where needed? Personal safety is a substantial issue for any community of discourse. If people don't feel safe, they won't enjoy the luxury of collaborating about other issues. You don't have worthwhile critical thinking without something substantial to think about. That's what you're providing for anyone who tries to hurt you or your loved ones.

"Perhaps you feel queasy, either about the gun, my arguments, or both. What's that? You think self-defense is justified under some circumstances, but the presence of the weapon in your community is a silent threat to use it? No one's forcing you to shoot anyone! I think this Russian gun was probably last owned by a Taliban rebel in Afghanistan, a Soviet soldier, or maybe both. But what does the history of the weapon matter anyway? That was somebody else's ethical worry.

"What's that? You're worried that weapons available in America are now more deadly and widespread? I agree. That's the very best reason for accepting my gift. If gun control crazies had their way, they'd make all law-abiding citizens surrender their guns. Talk about appeal to force! They can't get their opponents to agree with them, so they want regulations to punish them for disagreeing."

Write a five-page essay in which you show whether any of the arguments for or against gun control constitute an appeal to force. If you get to choose the disposition of your gift, what would you consider the most ethical course of action to take?

Would you return it, destroy it, learn how to use it, give it to someone else, or can you think of other possibilities?"

The appeal to force tricks us into mistaking a threat for an argument. But what is it about violence and terrorism which makes it appear to "succeed" for its perpetrators? Terrorism is purposive but terrorists do not wish to belong to anyone else's community of discourse. They want to undermine and manipulate those communities. Finding an ethical response to assaults upon communities is difficult. For example, read Alan Dershowitz's assessment of terrorism:

> "The reason terrorism works — and will persist unless there are significant changes in the responses to it — is precisely because its perpetrators believe that by murdering innocent civilians they will succeed in attracting the attention of the world to their perceived grievances and their demand that the world 'understand them' and 'eliminate their root causes'... We must commit ourselves never to try to understand or eliminate its alleged root causes, but rather to place it beyond the pale of dialogue and negotiation." — *Why Terrorism Works* (2002) by Alan M. Dershowitz

Dershowitz advocates responding to terrorism by refusing to enter into discourse with the terrorist. He insists that this is the only ethically appropriate way to think about terrorism. However, a community of discourse is also committed to the principle of scholarship. You can't deal effectively (or ethically) with something you do not genuinely understand. If Dershowitz is right that there is really nothing that needs or deserves to be understood about people willing to kill innocents, then our insistence on scholarship is misguided.

Share No. 35. You might not want to accept any gift from me about terrorism without having a bomb squad unwrap it first. Should we adopt the Dershowitz policy for the sake of preserving our own communities of discourse? Write an essay arguing for or against this position. Describe any two examples of terrorism from current events which you think support your answer.

G. The Sunburn Fallacy

Here is a fallacy for which we need to make up a name. We commit the *post hoc fallacy* by assuming that two events are related to each other as cause and effect simply because one closely follows the other. Chanticleer the rooster assumed that his crowing caused the sun to rise each morning. Philosopher David Hume argued that this assumption, which he called one of the principles of association, accounts for much of how we and other animals learn from experience. His works, *A Treatise of Human Nature* (1748) and *Enquiries concerning Human Understanding* (1739–1740) set forth the workings of these principles for epistemology. In the 20th century, psychology tried to make behavioral lemonade out this lemon of habitual associations by developing the theory of operant conditioning and ways of modifying reinforcement. But this robust joining of reliably successive events also makes us vulnerable to the post hoc fallacy. We could call this fallacy a built-in cost of a vigorous and often useful cognitive strategy of making associations.

This tendency to habitually associate conjoined experiences as cause and effect creates a sister fallacy which I dub "The Sunburn Fallacy." This is the fallacy of concluding that two events which we experience as significantly separated in time are therefore *not* related to each other as cause and effect. You've probably heard the hackneyed example of putting your hand on a hot stove as "learning from experience." Most of us concede that it must be real learning if we don't knowingly make that mistake twice. Lack of recidivism points to sincere and well-rooted learning about cause and effect.

On the other hand, how many people have been sunburned once and *only* once? We can experience the exposure to the sun and the later skin burn as sufficiently separated in time that our principle of association doesn't kick in. We know that the sun *causes* the burn, but we can easily act as though it doesn't. We feel stupid afterwards, but don't think of this fallacy as an ethical issue until we commit it in ways that affect others. For example, if you do work as a student or employee during a probationary period, and your efforts will not pay off until after the probationary period expires, it may be difficult for your teacher or employer to view the results as the effect of your work. In other words, if both events are not grasped as contiguous during your watch, a person can be vulnerable to the sunburn fallacy.

To take another example, if a climatologist demonstrates that merely sustaining current carbon emission levels will cause catastrophic climate changes by 2070, someone could acknowledge the causal connection, but still not experience it as a hot stove. It's not the absolute number of years between cause and effect which undermines our Principle of Association. Cities currently competing to host the Summer Olympics experience the connection between present activities and future outcome as robust. Instead of repeating or shouting the facts in angry frustration, we should find ways to change the "watch" or frame of reference so that cause and effect are experienced as conjoined.

We can be mature enough to understand that cause and effect don't always *feel* like cause and effect; but it's a hard lesson to learn. It runs counter to associative learning. One example that haunted me for years was the documentary account of the 1946 U.S. detonation of an atomic bomb at the Bikini Atoll in the Pacific. The Navy had ships stationed around the blast area to observe the spectacle ... really much too close to avoid dangerous radiation exposure. We can chalk that up to macho bravura in the face of danger, but it may also have been the old sunburn fallacy. The cause and effects of radiation may not be experienced as contiguous. They don't *feel* like cause and effect.

In these examples, the fallacy does create ethical issues of responsibility, duty, and attention to consequences of our actions. It's a fact that our successful strategies for understanding the world have this cognitive and motivational downside, but that doesn't make it a good excuse. The fact that we can't stand on our heads easily and for very long does not exempt us from trying when the stakes are high. Maybe we just need to achieve that posture long enough to "grasp" a connection that seems out of reach.

H. Fallacies Which Evolve, Stagnate, or Make Us Worry about Nothing

In textbooks, fallacies are separated out and each is identified with its own label. Outside textbooks, fallacies travel in packs. For that matter, people who hone and market fallacies also work in packs or teams. More recently, fallacies have been mutating like genetically engineered viruses which adapt, combine with other viruses and become even more virulent and resilient. Take racism as an example. This prejudice is stoked and relied upon in racist versions of the *ad hominem* fallacy. Racism can respond to social pressures, education, changes in laws, and even self-censorship without evaporating. Like a virus, it evolves to become more subtle, adaptive, systemic, and able to mask itself against being labeled "racism." The use of color evolves like a virus to link color to stigma or privilege in ways that are not blatant but are nevertheless potent. After a long career as a leading African-American historian and civil rights advocate, Prof. John Hope Franklin has no doubt seen his share of racist *ad hominem* attacks and is as much an authority as anyone on the subject. He argues that it is not color as such, but how we link color with rewards, assets, entitlements, and social attributes which allow racism cloud our thinking:

> "There is nothing inherently wrong with being aware of color as long as it is seen as making distinctions in a pleasant, superficial and unimportant manner. It is only when character is attached to color, when ability

is measured by color, when privilege is tied to color, and a whole galaxy of factors that spell the difference between success and failure in our society are tied to color—it is only when such considerations are attached to color that it becomes a deadly, dreadful, denigrating factor among us all...." — *The Color Line* by John Hope Franklin (1993)

Share No. 36 This is such a good argument from Franklin that it's a shame to use it only to deal with racism. So, use this present of scholarship in a new way. Take this quote from Prof. Franklin, and substitute for "color" words such as "age," "gender," "sexual orientation," or "disability." Write an essay which explains whether the argument still helps us to think clearly with these substitutions. Now take some riskier words such as "wealth," "beauty," or "education." In your essay, explain how the argument works or fails to work.

Not all fallacies cleverly adapt to stay alive and kicking. A fallacy can do just the opposite and justify lack of critical thinking in a community of discourse. Robert Grudin warns against what we might call the "fallacy of seniority" or the belief that you can expect to automatically know more, the longer you live:

"A monstrous fallacy of time, so ingrained that it is almost automatic, is the idea that we necessarily learn more and more about important human experiences as time passes. Born of the metaphor of childhood and maturity or of valid educational processes, this idea is then applied to areas where it has no validity at all — to love, morality, and politics, to art and self-knowledge. In these areas, it deludes us continually about our ability to deal with events, propelling us complacently into experiences which, to our surprise, turn out to be mystifying and new. Why do we so seldom increase our knowledge of these, the important human things? Because we learn only when we can accurately remember; and we can accurately remember only when we have accurately seen and heard; and our perception of crucial events is almost always so vain and superficial and riddled with fear that we carry away little of them except the tags and wrappers." — *Time and the Art of Living* by Robert Grudin (1982)

Robert Grudin turns our naïve correlation between age and knowledge upside-down. If he's right, it's a fallacy to suppose that time alone can be relied upon to give us any understanding if we don't practice real scholarship or are not willing to deal with matters of substance. A community of discourse tricked by this fallacy would be more likely to grow complacent and shallow over time instead of growing wise. For example, first year college students might learn much more in their first year of college than students in their senior year who commit the fallacy of believing that that they know more simply because they've been at college longer than the first year students.

Share No. 37 If you're in college, interview three first year students and invite them to honestly describe something important which they would like to know or understand better by the time they're seniors. Of course, this implies that your interviewees will admit to not knowing something which matters to them. The missing knowledge might be a kind of scholastic expertise or a revelation about what they want to do with their lives. Either way, this is knowledge for which they are waiting. Write up your findings. Next, interview three seniors and try to get them to honestly describe the most important things they have learned or understood in their four years of college. Is there anything which they think they might have understood better four years ago than they do now? Do your seniors seem pleased or disappointed about what they have learned or understood? If you're not in college, ask these questions first of three people much younger than yourself. Then ask the same questions of three people considerably older than yourself.

Few of us can claim to belong to optimal communities of discourse which are fallacy-free. What we do belong to are groups, some of which might be hospitable to new ideas. Only communities which are very intentional about applying the ethical principles for sustaining arguments have much chance of succeeding. But, given enough time, perhaps we will know enough to strengthen such communities. As a final test for thinking about matters of substance without fallacies, suppose that your community must think about ... nothing. However, there are silly, serious, meaningful, or difficult ways to think about nothing. Let's decide why, despite our collaboration, nothing has happened. Is there nothing to be done when we start shouting at each other? Someone makes an observation or offers an idea and the rest of us can think of nothing to say in response. Like nature, communities of discourse may need to restore themselves by lying fallow at times even though "nothing" seems to be happening. If you have a talkative group, you may not tolerate much silence, but that kind of "nothing" can be valuable at the right time.

Keeping in mind that you have nothing to lose and perhaps nothing to gain, read the following account of the USS Yorktown which was undone by the number zero. Let's call this "void where prohibited":

> "On September 21, 1997, while cruising off the coast of Virginia, the billion-dollar cruiser shuddered to a halt. USS Yorktown was dead in the water. Warships are designed to withstand the strike of a torpedo or the blast of a mine. Though it was armored against weapons, nobody had thought to defend the Yorktown from zero. It was a grave mistake. The Yorktown's computers had just received new software that was controlling the engines. Unfortunately, nobody had spotted the time bomb lurking in the code, a zero that engineers were supposed to remove ... When the Yorktown's computer system tried to divide by zero, 80,000 horsepower instantly became worthless. No other number

can do such damage." — *Zero — The Biography of a Dangerous Idea* by Charles Seife (2000)

Share No. 38 With the problems of forbidden knowledge or dangerous knowledge in mind, let's imagine a science fiction fantasy. Suppose that you're on a spaceship that encounters a planet with an intelligent non-human species called the *Plenitudians*. They have a socially advanced culture, arithmetic, and even astronomy, but they never discovered the idea of zero. If that's hard to imagine, consider that Europe got along on Roman numerals for centuries. The Plenitudians never discovered the concept of a vacuum either. Europe did not prove the existence of the vacuum until experiments in the 17th century. The Plenitudians see life and reality as quite full — a *plenitude*.

This culture is remarkably peaceful and intellectually vigorous. Their leading thinkers once considered the idea of zero but did not take it seriously. After all, concepts stand for real things. You don't need a concept to stand for nothing, do you? That would be a fantasy, not a concept. They also decided that the idea of "vacuum" or empty existence is a contradiction in terms. Sheer absence is not a rational concept for them. As good critical thinkers, they appreciate that you can't define something in strictly negative terms as the absence of something else. The Plenitudians have an enlightened relationship with other species of flora and fauna on their planet because they believe that every space must be occupied, and that all spaces are equal. As such, the very idea of making another species extinct or "nothing at all" is not only abhorrent to them, but literally unthinkable. There is no emptiness for the Plenitudians, only a world replete with life and full of ... well, fullness.

Ponder the Plenitudian paradise. Should you instruct them about vacuums and zeros? Expect the Plenitudians to immediately criticize the fallacy in your thinking. If you're thinking about zeros and vacuums, that's nothing, and thinking about nothing can't be taken seriously, they point out as they laugh

unkindly in your direction. Their most treasured work of litera-
ture is Fowler's *The Ethical Practice of Critical Thinking,* and
they zealously seek to argue only about matters of substance. As
such, Plenitudians would not waste their precious, precious time
debating the existence of nothing. Make a three-page case for
enlightening the Plenitudians, but in an ethically responsible
way. Then describe carefully and detail exactly how you would
teach them the meaning of zero or vacuum. Even though these
concepts are familiar, you will probably need to think carefully
and do some research to figure out how to communicate these
ideas to people who have never heard them. Where would you
begin? You need to be an effective scholar but also to convince
them that "nothing" really *is* a substantial issue. Good luck.

Chapter Four

The Ethical Practice of Doing the Math

A. Do the Math

If you are an individualist at heart who cherishes self-reliant thinking, you are probably getting annoyed and have only grudgingly tolerated the author's cant about collaboration and interdependence throughout the past three chapters. Now it's your turn to shine. Are you *tired* of all the value choices and relationship burdens demanded by critical thinking as an ethical practice? Would you like to kiss touchy-feely interdependence goodbye? What if you could put matters such as resolving festering conflicts and empathetically adopting another's perspective behind you with a clean conscience? You need only turn from words to numbers with which you can think autonomously, clearly, independently, decisively, and perhaps brilliantly. If anybody disagrees, tell them to do the math.[1]

---

1. Critical thinking texts often emphasize verbal thinking much more than thinking with numbers. Of course, mathematics deals with much more than integers, but numbers are a useful place to begin exploring math's ethical practice. A variety of disciplines are helpful here. For example, the sociology and anthropology of mathematics map and explain the relationships in which mathematical thinking is developed, rewarded, embedded, and applied, as well as cultural variances in mathematical systems. Math pedagogy has its own ethical challenges: Should we expect pure mathematics to have any ethical footprint? Is applied mathematics ethics-

Or so it seems. Mathematics enters collaborative thinking with its own agenda. Even logic is not so pushy.[2] Whether that agenda is intrinsic to numbers or to our culture of numbers is hard to say, but it might explain your (or your author's) math anxiety. That anxiety may not be entirely the fault of bad pedagogy or some shameful math ineptitude. Even bright people who like to calculate sense that mathematical reasoning, unlike verbal arguments, is more than a set of passive tools waiting to be used. Unlike words, numbers are much like a third party showing up to crash our party or abduct our community of discourse. So long as we stick to words, we can safely pretend that critical thinking is a quilt which we all sew or a game which we all play. We can choose among plenty of cooperative relational metaphors. But mathematical reasoning seeks

---

neutral regardless of the skills learned or their application? The code of ethics (2005) of American Mathematical Society deals primarily with plagiarism and related issues of research integrity among mathematicians. It does offer AMS support for "whistle-blowers" who assume risk in publicizing the social implications of certain mathematical research. Mathematical thinking is not the exclusive domain of mathematicians, however. Therefore, chapter four explores math as critical thinking and ethical practice.

2. I am dealing primarily with the limited mathematical task of calculation, but my quip about pushy math might seem biased against the more general logicist claim that mathematics can be reduced to logic. I don't think that we have to decide whether math or logic has the last word (or last symbol) to understand the compelling force of mathematical calculation. Mathematics and logic provide structures within and by means of which reasoning proceeds accurately or with the least ambiguity. Perhaps those virtues help us to experience those structures' boundaries as compelling. Rightly or wrongly, we see logic as a game, albeit a powerful one. In contrast, we externalize mathematical boundaries and limits as autonomous, final, and uncontestable courts of judgment. Perhaps we also expect logic to translate and clean up rather messy, incomplete, paradoxical, and ambiguous human cognition. We therefore know that something is lost in logic's translation. Though mathematics is a powerful language, we do not call upon it to translate nor do we dismiss it as a game. We differ about what to count, but we respect the bottom line.

and demands the correct answer, though it is admirably pluralistic about honoring different routes to the correct answer. Once we have that answer, the quilting bee screeches to a halt. The game is over. Although the profession of mathematics has a community of professional discourse, we have trouble finding or making such a community when we simply think mathematically together. What does "together" even mean for this kind of critical thinking? When we do math together at our table, does mathematics get its very own seat? If collaborative numerical reasoning might also be ethical practice, we need to figure out what sort of actual togetherness and relationships are at stake here.

> "This curious mathematical relationship widely known as the 'golden ratio,' was defined by Euclid more than two thousand years ago because of its crucial role in the construction of the pentagram, to which magical properties had been attributed. Since then it has appeared in the most astonishing variety of places—from mollusk shells, sunflower florets, and the crystals of some materials, to the shapes of galaxies. It has been asserted that the creators of the Pyramids and the Parthenon employed it...." — *The Golden Ratio—The Story of Phi, the World's Most Astonishing Number* by Mario Livio (2002)

Sometimes the "pushiness" of a mathematical relationship takes on a different sort of agenda as the focus of a numerology cult. Devotion to a mathematical relationship binds people together. Take the golden ratio, for example. Two quantities are in this ratio when the ratio between their sum and the larger quantity is equal to the ratio between the larger and smaller quantity. That's about 1.6180339887. Livio contends that admirers of the golden ratio have often fudged their math in their eager quest to "uncover" this ratio in nature, architecture and aesthetics. However, even if that ratio were accurately measured and reported, what ethical difference would the ratio make to how we treat each other? Perhaps this ratio unaccountably manifests itself as symbol or incarnation of a cosmic truth or as an answer to our need for a spiritual certainty and finality.[3] As esoteric as this peculiar preoccupation and collaboration may appear, it reflects a more fundamental and widespread human quest for balance, satisfying relationships, integration, and harmony. The quest may be para-religious, proto-ethical or simply religious on its own terms, but numerology's values are also shared by other types of collaboration which we would more readily recognize as ethical practice.

Share No. 39 Whether you're a teacher, student, employee, child, parent, spouse, friend, stranger, acquaintance, member, nonmember, junior, elder, insider, outsider, leader, or follower, you belong to certain relationships. But do you belong to *right* relationships, ethically speaking? Before you object that this is no math problem, think of geometry: Why does being inside or outside a social "circle" or drawing and crossing a moral "line" matter? Even children count and keep score on moral and social give-and-take. If you couldn't do math, or perhaps did a different sort of math, you might think differently about the rightness of relationships. Identify three important relationships or memberships which help to identify who you are. If you compare the rightness or wrongness of these relationships with some standard of a perfect relationship, figure out how much arithmetic, geometry, or algebra is involved, literally or metaphorically, particularly when people yearn for both sides to equal each other.

---

3. Like astrology, numerology tries to account for the normative or even sacred features of life through their association with mathematical qualities and relationships. To an outsider, a numerological system appears to argue in self-referential circles. Mathematicians may not be proud of their mystical heritage in numerological thinkers such as Pythagoras and Newton. Perhaps numerology makes us uncomfortable not because its supernatural speculations taint mathematics, but because numerology celebrates mathematics' old worship of perfect numbers and geometric solids. If we could wipe out or bracket this ancient idolatry, what sort of intuitive authority would remain for mathematical reasoning? When is an appeal to mathematics' authority legitimate and when is it a fallacy?

Do the numbers show that you are important or insignificant? Equal or unequal? Central or marginal? Remember, no one tries to improve a perfect relationship, but is an ethical relationship anything like finding the golden ratio?

Again, we seem to treat mathematics as a third party and not just as a shared set of skills. It's also an ancient example of what counts for us as objective truth or perfection. Since Plato, integers and geometric solids seemed incorruptible and unchanging embodiments of truth beyond subjectivity and opinion. For moderns, these truths might no longer be counted upon to deliver goodness or beauty. Yet, we hold the numbers to be free of ethical prescriptions, human values, prejudices, biases, and conflicts of interest. In fact, speaking of "moral mathematics" is an unseemly oxymoron for us, because we still romanticize numbers as unchanging, unyielding, impartial, and indifferent participants in our thinking. Even as the fabric of critical thinking we don't suppose numbers or equations are hostage to our personal perspectives and subjective interpretations. For many of us, mathematical reasoning promises correct answers to well-defined problems.

Because we grant numbers this version of diplomatic moral immunity, we don't expect them to be dirtied with ethical accountability. We will admit that numbers may be victims of human wrongdoing when someone does deceptive tricks with numbers to dupe the unsuspecting. We acknowledge nasty things done with math. We just have a hard time believing that doing math necessarily involves the ways we treat each other. We didn't count on that.

B. I Am Not a Number!

On the other hand, let's expect that such an important part of human cognition as mathematical reasoning is likely to be wrapped up in choices of values and it's bound to affect how we treat each other. For example, the 20th century bemoaned the prospect of human beings being reduced to numbers. The phrase "I am not a number!"

is from a 1960's British science-fiction spy series called "The Prisoner." I grew up watching this show. A British secret agent resigned from the Secret Service and was abducted to an isolated resort village. In this village, he is merely "No. 6" and, he is treated with unctuous solicitude and sinister bonhomie while being interrogated by each episode's new "No. 2." Those in charge won't tell No. 6 why they want information, which side they're on, or the identity of No. 1. He is now merely a number. We never learn his name.

There's a popular style of cosmology which intones that we are but one planet amidst billions of galaxies in order to induce wonder, humility, or despair (take your pick). On the other hand, we use numbers to bolster our importance. We predictably aspire to the best spot in whatever cardinal ordering system declares us to be No. 1, and we subordinate ourselves and each other to quantitative demands, risking considerable moral disrespect of each other. The math itself remains irreproachable, however, because when we argue with each other, we won't argue easily about the numerical order we've invented and adopted.

How we think about numbers creates opportunities for moral metaphors and analogies too. In her book, *Aftermath,* Susan Brison uses the mathematical concept of a "surd" to explain the moral challenge of incorporating a violent trauma into ones view of the world. Just as a surd contains the root of an irrational number that can never be expressed or integrated successfully into a series of rational or whole integers, so trauma has the same unyielding resistance being tamed, framed, and wedged into our understanding of personal relationships.

It is a common complaint that people can't easily understand the significance of very large or very small numbers. When the large number refers to genocide, the lack of understanding is ethically distressing. We reason that our moral outrage about any serial or mass killing should increase in proportion to the number of victims. At best, we strive for awe, sober respect, or commensurate humility when bludgeoned by integers with many zeros. However, we do handle the significance of large or small integers when there is a sustaining argument at stake. Tell me that I may spend a million dollars in thirty days, and the zeros are no problem. We try graphic pie charts and analogies. The inspiring "paper clips" project of Whitwell Middle School began as a class project to convey to students the numerical scope of the Holocaust. The morally and spiritually inspiring aspect of the story is not the sheer number of clips which the students managed to receive and store from around the world, but the ethical relationships with others, including Holocaust survivors that were formed as a result of counting with diligence as a community responsibility. Watch the documentary "Paper Clips!"

On a lighter note, I once had a friend who complained that the local traffic light was timed wrong for the neighborhood intersection it directed, causing needless waits. Nothing came of his rant until he finally sat down at the intersection for a few days and timed the lights, counted the vehicles, and presented his findings to the City Council. They couldn't dispute the findings, so they fixed the light. If you think that math doesn't matter to ethics, sit in your car at an intersection for no good reason other than the fact that nobody had yet bothered to count for you.

Share No. 40 There is something in your community which remains sadly under-counted or under-measured. What have you noticed increase or decrease that caused you concern for the loss of a value, an unmet need, or a potential danger? On the bright side, what increase or decrease has given you hope, comfort, or delight? Do the math and find out exactly how much, how long, and at what rate. Then share your findings with the community which has a substantial interest in what you confirmed and can act on it. Report the results.

Twenty years ago, Douglas Hofstadter (and later John Allen Paulos) decried the modern failing of "innumeracy" or numerical il-

---

4. Massimo Piattelli-Palmarini's *Inevitable Illusions* (1994) argues that we have innate and irreversible cognitive illusions in our reasoning about

literacy.[4] This is lack of skill in reasoning with numbers or handling mathematical concepts. Strangely, when we lack competence using and interpreting mathematics, we're not as ashamed about this incompetence as we would be about being labeled "illiterate." For example, our poor intuition about understanding very large or very small numbers or how to correctly assess probability should make our conscience twinge as we fumble like self-conscious children failing to solve problems at the blackboard as the consequences of these figures and our own poor ability to cope with them accumulate. The reformist platform does have an ethical plank.

Can we still justifiably believe that, unless we're crunching numbers for an evil person or using math skills to do something wicked, math itself is ethics-neutral and ethics-free? Let's apply our four principles of ethical arguments (charitable interpretation, scholarship, substance, and conflict) and the four associated skills (objectivity, curiosity, suffering, and sufficiency) where they're most needed.

We could start by applying the **principle of charitable interpretation**: and choose the most plausible interpretation of the arguer's mathematical reasoning and the best reasoning to be found in those calculations. We can be very individualistic and uncharitable about

---

matters of quantity, particularly concerning probability, which are independent of intelligence and education (pp. 139–140). This approach might make us pessimistic about collaboration in mathematical thinking if that reasoning is unavoidably undermined by illusions. For example, if I'm doomed to commit the gambler's fallacy, does that excuse me from gambling away my family's savings? Pessimism may be premature. We might praise a critical thinker who navigates sagely, patiently, and humbly around such illusions. If an illusion is truly general, this egalitarian assumption could incline us to forgive even an otherwise capable thinker whose illusions lead her to act upon fallacies. We may expect her to apologize and repair any harm she caused. We help or harm each other in ways that we can't avoid or don't intend, but that doesn't end our relationships, our responsibilities in those relationships, or our respect and concern for others.

mathematical thinking. Part of this comes from the perfectionist discipline of mathematics itself. We don't have as much empathy for dyscalculia as we might for dyslexia. But the rest is simply a lack of charity in reasoning together. Simply intoning "Do the math" does not settle ethical questions. For example, if you assert that the normal human body temperature is 98.6 ° F. (37.0 C) then it may frustrate you to discover that any temperature between 97.6° and 98.8° F. is normal. Not only do we demand more precision out of temperature than it can deliver, we use this as a pretext to demand it from each other.

The skill of objectivity still matters, though *how* we know something may be disciplined as much by the language of mathematics itself as by the quantitative demands of what we think about. For example, objective calculation involves the skill of counting, knowing what to count, and what the actual relationship of the counting task is to related domains. By the way, I am convinced that mathematics has gotten a bum rap for being cold, petty, and impersonal. If what you count doesn't "count" in any meaningful human way, then perhaps it is you who want to be cold and petty or have chosen to relate to others impersonally. Quantitative thinking can have brighter and warmer ethical colors in the right hands. You may decide to tabulate what is worth counting, measure with care to minimize mistakes and maximize fairness, help others to grasp substantive quantitative facts, cope with and predict change, or provide discipline necessary to making ethical decisions about resources.

C. All Other Things Being Equal

If we do our critical thinking about some causal relationship which is embedded in a system of self-contained or merely contingent relationships, we can confidently test and identify that causal relationship, *ceteris paribus* ("all other things being equal"). When we think about a relationship between a disease and its cause in the complex and highly interdependent systems such as the human body, we need medical skill to utter *ceteris paribus* with credibility. Perhaps the way we test linear cause and effect relationships in a system is a useful analogy for how we test our critical thinking in our ethical practice. In systems which are morally dense, highly interdependent, and in which decision-making is urgent, we utter *ceteris paribus* only with discretion, humility, and care. This is so regardless of whether we think with arguments or equations. What if we must deliver hard truths or respect cold and unforgiving numbers? At the very least, we should not pretend that the inferences or conclusions of our critical thinking are hard, cold, or unforgiving. If we choose to be judgmental, let's not make logic or math the scapegoat.

One important application of *ceteris paribus* in our ethical practice is the task of risk assessment. When I reason, "All other things being equal, this is an acceptable risk," I invoke the mathematics of probability, the sociology of consensus, and some ethical baggage that I ought to claim. There's my conviction that it's wrong to harm others, all other things being equal, but also my romantic conceits about fate and fortune, along with my hard-won philosophy of life grounded in certainty that living with zero risk is impossible and therefore some risk is necessary. We can make the critical thinking less personal by participating in a community of discourse trying to ascertain acceptable risk in a new drug. At our table, we seek consensus among scientists, doctors, lawyers, government officials, and stockholders. There's only one empty chair left at the table. Shall we offer it to a future patient or to the theory of probability?

We may be more likely to make more mathematical errors outside our evolutionary calculation comfort zone, but we don't act more *unethically* just because we must assess quantitative relationships in unusual or unfamiliar territory. Measurement, calculation, and grasping ratios are mindful and exacting ways of thinking critically about the world. If you relate to me in ways that are calculating, that doesn't make our relationship brutal or lacking in compassion. If you value your calculation more than you value others, then ethical practice is threatened. Adhering to your best quantitative thinking is a matter of integrity, not detachment or indifference to ethics. You may not be able to do the right thing until you can stand by or acknowledge the right answer. If our relationship is entirely new or novel for you, you can at least be kind to strangers or in situations which are strange to you.

Think about lightning. Does it matter? The National Lightning Safety Institute advises that, "if the earth's surface beneath a storm cloud were perfectly flat, lightning could be expected to strike any point on the earth with equal probability."[5] Equal probability in that mathematical Flatland might justify our becoming placid or paranoid. Either way, we want to live rightly with each other because we all face the same odds. In our non-Flatland we think as carefully about the risks of lightning as our ethical practice demands. Notwithstanding that people typically die from causes other than lightning, our best assessment of risk is one of our best ways of caring for each other. The fact that a given lightning strike is random and unpredictable doesn't eclipse our ethical responsibility for coping with the possibility of such strikes. Only a thousand out of 280,000,000 Americans were struck by lightning last year. That doesn't make victims' suffering inconsequential. Some of us have a greater tolerance or appetite for risk than do others, but accepting or imposing a risk is an ethical practice—a practice which matters for people who should matter to each other. The story goes that a Presbyterian church would not use a lightning rod offered by Ben Franklin because God would never smite their congregation. Franklin noted that they kept their roof repaired lest they be smitten by God's raindrops. If lightning statistics are, well, damning enough to make you reluctant to play golf in Florida around

5. The National Lightning Safety Institute is a nonprofit non-advocacy organization dedicated to the mitigation of lightning damage. Its founder, Richard Kithill, Jr., is an international consultant on lightning safety.

4:00 p.m. in July, how you put that probability to use says more about your ethical practice than it does about fate or divine wrath. Ethical practices required by critical thinking in a community of discourse do presume at least enough normalcy to build and sustain a community of this kind, whether it's good manners or good ethics that make up the normalcy. Keeping promises, listening with respect, honoring duties, and upholding the group's values matter as ongoing concerns. What about shocking and unexpected incidents? Though crises are infrequent, virtually by definition, that doesn't make them irrelevant for critical thinking or for ethical practice. Similarly, if we can prove that a certain event is mathematically improbable for our community, that doesn't make it negligible or insignificant, however unlikely it may be. Whether we happen to do our best or our worst critical thinking under pressure, and regardless of whether we nobly reaffirm or sadly betray our ethics in times of crisis, those junctures are as much a part of our critical thinking together as are the more comfortable and nurturing times.

Whether we find our community caught in crisis or carrying on business as usual, we might succumb to biases about which numbers we should take seriously. For example, if we agree that the odds of being killed by walking to a destination as opposed to driving are much lower; will we straightaway sell our cars? If we agree that we can all significantly increase the odds of living longer by consuming no more than 1500 calories per day, who will dare to order the group's next lunch?

Even if we diligently train against or scrub away biases in our critical thinking, some spots apparently won't come out if Massimo Piattelli-Palmarini is correct in *Inevitable Illusions*. If he's right that we reason poorly in ways that can be attributed to verified cognitive illusions, then we're stuck with them as part of the human condition. By way of contrast, Dietrich Dönner's *The Logic of Failure* (1989) shifts our attention from inescapable illusions to unavoidable perils of system complexity, but he guides managers to navigate through them successfully. On the other hand, we might dispense with the putative phenomena of robust and inexpugnable fallacies and cognitive illusions by giving the mind credit for some discerning skills such as the ability to distinguish between the probabilities of frequencies and single events, as argued by Gerd Gigerenzer.[6] The empirical evidence that evolution has wired human cognition against being mired in systemic irrationality is not exactly overwhelming, but we can still count our evolutionary blessings. We just need to remember that irrationality, like lightning, can be expected to strike twice in certain places.

D. Fairness as a Math Skill

Sustaining arguments prove something worth discussing, allow decisions worth considering, or lead to commitments worth making. We can achieve this by applying the **principle of substance:** choose only matters and issues for arguments which deserve our best thinking, facilitate necessary decisions, and in which there are stakes that matter for the benefit or detriment of all concerned. You would need to know which measurements matter most for the group. For example, if you can't make numbers or mathematical procedures meaningful, then a scholarship responsibility has not been fulfilled. A necessary skill for practicing this principle is **suffering**. That's a special dilemma when dealing with equations. Call it the

---

6. See Gigerenzer, G. "How to Make Cognitive Illusions Disappear: Beyond Heuristics and Biases." *European Review of Social Psychology* 2: 83–115 (1991).

7. How we suffer or are consoled by presumably meaningful numbers and equations doesn't necessarily match all mathematical expectations. For example, we can suffer from gaining half a pound while remaining unfazed by genocide statistics. Suffering is not directly proportional to quantity. Before we moralize about our compassion or indifference, we should examine how we actually treat each other in response to the mathematical facts we learn.

phenomenological challenge of reconciling our suffering with the mathematical facts we learn.[7] It's remarkable how much we rely upon mathematical measures and concepts to define or assess the fairness of a situation. Just as we live in an economy that can measure financial value in terms of time saved, spent, or invested, so modern penology measures punishment in terms of time imposed, deprived, or reprieved. Certainly, it's hard to imagine distributive justice or reparation without measurement. In retributive justice, doing the math is tantamount to doing fairness. Algebra has no greater demand for balance than our hunger for commensurate payback for crimes.

What about conflicts? Sustaining arguments strengthen a community as it confronts and learns from the conflicts, impasses, failures, and sacrifices which are part of arguing together as a community. We can achieve this by applying the **principle of conflict**. Recall that a community is sustained by the way that it handles its conflicts in argument. A necessary skill to apply this principle is that of **sufficiency**. That's the skill of knowing when "enough is enough" and a conflict cannot usefully move further without major changes.

We don't typically tolerate value-laden conflict *within* mathematical thinking since we don't expect to find moral conflict as part of measuring or verifying quantitative relationships. Quantitative research can be politically or socially provocative, but such collaboration assumes, to some extent, that the single right or best answer will emerge, regardless of the mathematical method which uncovers it. This one-answer expectation can favor perfectionism in ethical practice, and that is not particularly compatible with charitable interpretation.

"What is most shocking about America's reaction to Turkey's killing of Armenians, the Holocaust, Pol Pot's reign of terror, Iraq's slaughter of the Kurds, Bosnian Serbs' mass murder of Muslims, and the Hutu elimination of Tutsi is not that the United States refused to deploy U.S. ground forces to combat the atrocities … What is most shocking is that U.S. policymakers did almost nothing to deter the crime … The key question after a century of false promise, is: Why does the United States stand so idly by?" —*A Problem From Hell: America and the Age of Genocide* by Samantha Power (2002)

You may present such grim and incontrovertible figures to your community only to find that they elicit no commensurate response of outrage, urgency, or altruism. They are free to morally respond, but they do not. They don't dispute the figures but find no binding loyalty or moral sentiment compelling them to any immediate response beyond sighing with sad resignation or resentfully grousing "What do you expect us to do about it?" "Enough is enough" does not mean that your facts should carry their own moral banner. "Enough is enough" does not mean that your crusade has failed because your expectations are disappointed. Learning the skill of sufficiency is successfully applying Aristotle's "golden mean" to shape practice rather than virtue. Or moral persuasion's sufficiency may be to gently reach a "tipping point" at which people begin to rally in useful ways. Whatever the best metaphor for sufficiency happens to be, it is worthwhile to ask what is really missing from the situation besides your gratified expectations.

Share No. 41 When we apply the skill of sufficiency to punishment, the modern system of criminal justice and incarceration regularly determines "enough is enough" for social retribution. In fact, criminal justice is almost essentially a math problem when you consider the quantitative format of most sentencing grids. You can find plenty of examples in criminal justice texts or by looking at such grids online. Here are a few current sites:

http://images.morris.com/images/cjonline/mdControlled/cms/2007/07/01/181312192.jpg

http://www.co.lane.or.us/DA/images/GridFront.gif

You will easily recognize that the numerical system and graphics of the Periodic Table of Elements is used for many such grids. The criminal charges are alphabetized and color-coded in the same way.

Here's your Share No. 41. Design your own sentencing grid. However, in the place of jail terms for the offender, insert reparation and restoration amounts for the victims of these crimes. If you want to stick to time, decide how long the State or the community is sentenced to take care of the victim's needs and in what ways. You may have a problem identifying victims for certain crimes, but do your best. Then show your grid to three crime victims whom you know and find out their assessments of your grid. Write their evaluation on the back of your grid and respond to them in writing.

Share No. 42 We recognize that words can heal, but we don't give numbers credit for having this quality even though honoring special numbers is part of many cultures. A group's celebration of special numbers is not numerology. Numbers may not be justice, but, like words, they can symbolize justice, celebration, or community. When families measure a child's height with pencil notches on the wall or birthdays, the numbers are a way of showing that the child matters. The cardinal ordering of anniversaries does this for relationships.

You may know a person or group that is under-appreciated. Come up with a new *mathematical* celebration for them. It has to be a meaningful calculation which will achieve the healing, support, and affirmation. Stage the celebration and then describe the event in a three-page essay which you share with others. If the person or group can suggest numbers which matter to them, that should give you a clue as to what to measure.

Share No. 43 Horrible skills such as expertly torturing children are always immoral, but the medieval church prohibited the seemingly benign skill of calculating and charging loan interest. The mathematical and financial practice was deemed not simply unwise or burdensome for Christians to impose upon the debtor. The very practice of using interest calculation was morally condemned as *usury*. Mathematics frames and empowers certain financial practices. As a creditor, whether you consider a loan arrangement usurious would differ according to your culture's laws and religion. The debtor might judge usury based upon personal resources. For example, let's say that I accept your $1,000.00 loan to me at 5% interest. The agreement includes the formula for periodic compound interest, but it gives you discretion to alter the period. Yes, 5% compounded annually would be nothing compared to 5% compounded monthly. By changing the formula, you could keep me poor indefinitely as you get richer. Does the ethical stink of your mathematic tweaking smell any better because I agreed to be bound by your "discretion" in the loan terms?

Here's your task. If you have a credit card, a loan, mortgage, or lease, give the documents outlining the terms of the agreement information to a friend, along with a calculator, and let him or her do the consumer math and find out what this loan arrangement actually costs you until the loan is repaid. Do the same for one of your friend's financial arrangements. Consider yourselves a small but earnest financial community of discourse. Report your findings to each other in an essay and decide whether the arrangement raises issues not just of prudence or ignorance about the morality of the financial relationship.

Share No. 44 (Optional) Here's a parting math share. Your author could not resist a word problem. Let's say that you began this chapter by understanding 50% of the ethical problems caused by mathematical reasoning. By now, you have understood an additional 20% of those ethical problems. However, when you rush out and buy the improved and surprisingly affordable 2nd edition of my book, your understanding will increase an additional 30%. What is the final amount of ethical problems that you will then understand? Please do not make any extraneous pencil markings on this page. Do your ethical and math calculations on scrap paper.

Is your ethical practice directly proportional, inversely pro-
portinal, unrelated, or otherwise related to the amount of ethical problems which you understand? give your reasons and do
the math.

Chapter Five

Finding a Community of Discourse

You may be getting very tired of this puppy. But you can't think critically about him without raising ethical issues. When you do any thinking that matters to you (and to anyone else), when you think with curiosity, objectivity, and a keen appreciation of how numbers help and hurt, you uncover plenty of ethical issues along the way. What you uncover are not just ethical items that you snag in the course of thinking about something—they're the very ethical features of thinking itself. This running gag of the adorable puppy is here to remind us that even the most abstruse or self-absorbed critical thinking is not ethics-neutral, ethics-free or ethics-contrary. You sail into critical thinking and wind up in ethics. While it would be much simpler to keep critical thinking a matter of learning about logic and fallacies without worrying about collaboration with other thinkers, our best critical thinking about things which matter means that this puppy follows us.

We can sort the psyche into separate compartments of cognition, motivation, judgment, and behavior for purposes of knowledge about the psyche, but not for purposes of living. We live and think critically through relationships with the world and with each other. Perhaps we can understand the relationship between critical thinking and ethical practice with better metaphors. Critical thinking casts long ethical shadows, displays bright ethical colors, and it packs a hefty ethical mass. We're also willing to use critical thinking as a new broom to sweep clean ethical confusion and clutter. Metaphors aside, you might not be convinced that being ethical necessarily makes you a better critical thinker. But we can argue that the most productive and disciplined thinking typically demands ongoing collaboration and certain kinds of sustained human relationships. In other words, thinking critically happens as an ongoing ethical practice, whether we're saints or scamps.

Oddly, we still *resent* ethics and morality pushing critical thinking around. Thinking is about autonomy, independence, intellectual sovereignty and truth, or at least, that's our favorite part of its story. However, if resentment is refusal to be held accountable for how our thinking damages or helps others, then our sovereign ship is sunk, to borrow W.K. Clifford's metaphor.[1] On the other hand, keeping ethics at arm's length from critical thinking can also keep

---

1. Philosopher W.K. Clifford's famous essay, *The Ethics of Belief* (1877) argues that holding an unjustified belief exposes one to moral censure. For example, suppose a ship-owner reasonably doubts the safety of his ship but talks himself out of his doubts and allows the ship to sail. The ship sinks and all aboard die. Was his belief morally negligent or was the *action based on that illegitimate belief* negligent, or both? Risk assessment is more problematic than this (no pun intended), but Clifford makes his point that belief is not entirely private nor is the way we adopt beliefs beyond praise or blame as part of our shared ethical practice. The essay was originally published in Contemporary Review (1877), was reprinted in Lectures and Essays (1879) and can presently be read in various ethics an-

us from understanding and practicing critical thinking at its best, in collaboration, scholarship, despite conflict, and about matters which matter. In short, sealing off critical thinking from any contact with ethics makes critical thinking conventional, mediocre, and possibly dangerous. So, if you're reasonably assured that ethics won't necessarily taint or shackle your critical thinking, let's explore this issue further.

Ethics also means acquiring virtues, committing to values, upholding rights, choosing or accepting duties, making free and sometimes risky choices, developing empathy, and doing all that in a web of social relationships, knowing that you'll eventually die (Deadlines motivate people, don't they?). So, doing critical thinking isn't just following a set of rules. Even if it were, how would you react to a student—or a computer—who claimed to have generated an absolute ethical truth from such a set of rules? You'd probably object, "Who's to say?" or point out that there's no absolute standard of right and wrong that everyone agrees upon, or that even intelligent and well-intentioned people can't agree about ethics, especially if the issues involved are controversial.

Oh, we almost forgot ... there remains that inescapable and now critically underfed puppy banished from its loving home and facing imminent starvation because you said that you wanted to keep critical thinking detached, private, and uninvolved. "Who's to say?" Well, *you* said, and now you have to deal with it.

A. Letting Sleeping Dogs Starve

Hopefully, you've been convinced that the techniques of critical thinking are useful. But you may need further convincing that you should expect critical thinking to lead you into ethical issues

thologies, and in *The Ethics of Belief and Other Essays* (Promethius Books, 1999).

and moral responsibilities. Even if you relent and don't throw away this book out of charity to the author, you might still find that a good software program can give you plenty of practice learning logic and sharpening your analytic skills. Isn't that all that critical thinking is about?

Think again. As we've learned in a variety of contexts, the missing element is the *social* nature of thinking implied by what you've learned about critical thinking thus far. Whether you're a student, lawyer, doctor, scientist, or business professional, you think not just by trying to reason soundly or picking apart bad arguments. You also practice scholarship as you question, research, discover, and confirm whether an argument's premises really *are* true.

In real life, premises aren't pre-labeled as "true" or "false" as they are in critical thinking exercises. These practices of discovering and confirming are partially about figuring out whom and what to trust, and under what conditions. It's a social quest. Hopefully, your author, teacher, and fellow critical thinkers will partner with you in this quest. Propositions have more than a truth value. They also have a history. Arguments have more than conclusions. They also have a very human audience with its own foibles. Even with the best standards to guide us, we find that bias, error, laziness, secrecy, and dishonesty can undermine our scholarship quest, just as diligent intelligence, and honest collaboration can improve scholarship.

B. Loyalty Oath

So, we form communities to uphold standards appropriate to the kind of evidence and arguments which matter to us, such as science or journalism, and which will prevent or at least help to correct our most likely intellectual vices and failings. This is how we endeavor to keep each other honest about what we know and what we don't know. Sometimes, we make use of the community at hand: our friends and acquaintances. We can call these *discourse communities* or what philosopher Jürgen Habermas termed *communities of discourse,*[2] and developed a discourse ethics emphasizing ethical principles such as freedom, equality, and solidarity for the common good. It's being in community that introduces us to certain ethical responsibilities and obligations pertinent to critical thinking.

"You all know that if a club or a sect is to be begun ... two things are necessary: first a leader, or a group of leaders, eager, enthusiastic, convinced, or, at the worst, capable of speaking as if they were convinced — leaders persistent, obstinate, and in their own fitting way aggressive; and, secondly, a cause that can be idealized so that, when the leaders talk of it in their glowing exhortations, it seems to be a sort of supernatural being ... The two aspects of loyalty, the personal and the seemingly superpersonal, must thus be emphasized together."
The Philosophy of Loyalty **by Josiah Royce (1908)**[3]

Philosopher Josiah Royce claimed that loyalty to any club fails un-

---

2. A non-metaphorical way of closely linking critical thinking with ethical practice is Habermas' *A Theory of Communicative Action* (1981). Habermas deals with the ethical presuppositions of rational communication. For example, he notes the presuppositions that relevant arguments are not suppressed and that force is not used against the participants except for the "force" of the better argument. Though I'm not convinced that bona fide critical thinking requires pure motives or a single purpose, my emphasis upon the four principles of sustaining arguments follows a similar strategy though with many metaphors. However, Habermas' political and sociological analysis of meaningful communication in the public sphere goes far beyond the modest interpersonal relationships at the core of my book. The ways in which ideology and social forces shape ethical practice and the very possibility of meaningful critical thinking are absent in *The Ethical Practice of Critical Thinking*. Whether that absence makes this text's approach unrealistic or simply incomplete is a valid question, but I think such relationships can teach us on their own terms about critical thinking at its best. I'm content that critical thinking finds its rightful place in the moral universe without trying the more strenuous task of generating the moral universe out of communicative action.

3. Royce's lectures on loyalty were long out of print but can now be found through Kessinger Publishing (2004) online at JSTOR, and else-

less it's also "loyalty to loyalty itself"—a local dedication which nurtures deeper dedication and loyalties in a community. Otherwise, a particular loyalty becomes divisive, competitive, or an unsupportable fixation in a changing world. That raises the question about the loyalties of a fledgling community of discourse. It's not quite a club or a sect. The group is loyal to working together on whatever sustaining arguments are most pressing, and the group is loyal to treating each other with the respect necessary for being such a community. I hope that's not too circular. If you have nothing to contribute to a given topic or dislike someone in the group, that shouldn't count as disloyalty to the community. However, if you demean the other participants, offer only sloppy reasoning and fabricated evidence, or else gossip so much that no argument can be sustained, then that amounts to disloyalty, as Royce would say. You are no longer loyal to your community's loyalty: helping each other to think about and through a topic.

That doesn't mean that taking a pessimistic view of the topic or of the possibilities of the group is necessarily disloyal. Consider:

> **"Declinist works get much of their rhetorical force from contrasting an idealized past, its vices overlooked, with a demonized present, its virtues overlooked ... The genre's most distinctive feature is the assumption of cultural unity—the mutual dependence of the various departments of culture in a broadest sense... ."**—*Public Intellectuals—A Study of Decline* by Richard Posner (2001)

What community of discourse would be complete without a Jeremiah? Like the ancient prophet Jeremiah, these critical thinkers view culture as a fragile resource which can be lost as a result of

---

where. Royce did not foresee loyalty's ghastly collaboration with ideology, war, and genocide in the 20th century. Sadly, our loyalties don't answer the question "What should matter most?" Loyalties indicate how we succeed or fail to answer the question. Perhaps loyalties can become so grand and noble (or so base and dehumanizing) that the word "loyalty" no longer does justice to our attachments, whether transcendent or unspeakable.

single disagreeable trend, thereby abandoning a golden age for a future of chaos, barbarism, and general nastiness. Some contemporary public intellectuals, such as Gertrude Himmelfarb, Alan Bloom, Tim LaHaye, Robert Bork, or Christopher Lasch have become famous for taking on this role. Consider your group's Jeremiah as a reality check to keep you honest about progress and possibilities. Watch out for assuming too much cultural unity. Your community's culture may be more modular. It may be sinking in one area while buoyant or rising in other areas.

Of course, we do plenty in discourse communities besides practice critical thinking, but how we choose to argue is an underappreciated part of whether we live well together. How and whether people actually manage to come together to argue, whether our arguments or problem-solving actually help or hurt anyone, and whether our communities are stronger or weaker as a result of those arguments are important ethical questions. So, as we do critical thinking, we find ourselves also entering into certain ethical relationships, not just by accident, but because of what the discipline of critical thinking demands of us. We should be ready for these relationships.

For example, arguing, when it's done in good faith and with mutual respect, is one way we help each other to think, even if we don't convince others that we're right. We argue in earnest to convey that the topic at hand is worth our sustained attention. The discipline of putting our claims and assertions into words for others and discovering where our propositions lead us makes it easier for others to think about issues more clearly. Real arguments, unlike those in textbook exercises, do not exist as unchanging, fully formed, and polished intellectual products suitable for thinking. They have to get started, which can be messy and risky.

Share No. 45 Take it upon yourself to convince your group that it has a mission, duty, and priority to discuss and resolve a particular issue which the majority regards as an "inconvenient topic." It's substantial, urgent, and your community is nevertheless completely opposed to considering it. Yet their failure to do so will send your community to hell or thereabouts, with or without a hand basket. They wouldn't accept this share of yours even as a gift. It will take some convincing. Your group may find some other issue more germane to their particular needs and interests. Take on the honorable though thankless role of Jeremiah and don't let this pressing issue be shelved, tabled, or postponed. Once they have argued about this as well as they can muster, then they may return to their other issues. Explain which topic you championed, your reasons, and any sustaining arguments which emerged. Let's hope they eventually thank you before they stone you.

Once it gets started, the argument develops as it meets objections, or is refuted. This development is only possible in social relationships of give and take. This is why developing any worthwhile argument means that you're also making some basic ethical choices about showing respect, maintaining integrity, engaging in conversation, and possibly manifesting virtues such as courage just for getting the new argument off the ground—even if the topic is initially difficult or not entirely welcomed by the group.

C. *Nobody* Expects the Community of Discourse!

Suppose that you've just enrolled in college. You meet another new student named Jason during orientation week. He doesn't obviously have any traits or background in common with you, so, as you chat about the routine of getting settled on campus, it seems that he'll be just one more name to remember. Apart from the fact that the two of you enrolled in the same college, you can't latch onto any fact about this guy with which to form a relationship. You can't even think of much else to say to him.

Just as you're about to break off the conversation, you hear him mention a topic that you really care about. Perhaps you can't tell whether Jason is an expert on the subject, but he clearly cares about this subject which also happens to matter very much to you. The conversation now becomes exciting, not just because you discovered a common interest, but because you both care more about the topic than your own egos. You're not just swapping information. You're creating an intellectual partnership. You are also creating different kinds of respect. You can't continue to respect the topic's urgency, complexity, or depth unless you and Jason also respect each other's intelligence and difference in perspectives. Your new intellectual partnership, ushers you into new ethical obligations, not just to be diligent about the topic you both love to discuss, but also diligent about respecting each other in argument. That's not a bad way to begin a friendship either.

D. Community Crashers

Have you ever been having an extremely interesting discussion with friends about an issue you care about, only to have someone barge into the conversation by belittling people, using sarcasm, or interrupting people who are talking? Worse yet, this person derails the group's argument by attacking the speaker or pandering to the group's prejudices to make a point. Bad arguments, like bad manners, lower the standard of discourse and tend to undermine mutual trust and respect. When a bad argument causes you to lose trust and respect for your own thinking or that of others, the argument has failed you, not just because of faulty logic, but by using argument to undermine your responsibilities and values.

Sometimes we think through things on our own, and, at other times, we confer with others. Either way, critical thinking doesn't happen in a social vacuum. It's always a public responsibility because the arguments we come up with, whether on our own or in collaboration with others, influence how we behave and how others think too.

Arguments can inflict minor harm when they are petty or pointless and can do major harm too. Imagine someone with a valid and sound argument on a worthwhile topic who deploys it against others in such a mean-spirited, abusive, and hateful way that the whole exercise makes it harder for that community to engage in further discussion and argument on that or any other topic.

The problem with our malicious arguer isn't that he is "merely being honest" or "only telling the truth" or even that he's tactless. The problem is that our arguer lacks an awareness of relationship with others. Our merely honest and only truthful debater hurls his argument like a note in a bottle which has been tossed into the ocean for anybody or nobody to retrieve, or perhaps more like a Molotov cocktail tossed into a crowd.

E. The Cost of Community of Discourse

If critical thinking and ethical practice were combined in a chemistry experiment, which would be the solution and which would be the precipitate? So far, we've sloshed critical thinking vigorously and ethical practice is the precipitate which settles the bottom of our beaker. How much precipitate is optimal? We've already discussed possible standards of principles and ethical skills. In the real world, just how do you find a real community of discourse? If you want to start one, it's certainly more than picking a topic or issue and hashing out our attitudes and opinions about it with a random collection of people. As soon as we start thinking and arguing in earnest, we discover in doing so that we are in relationship to each other, and not just to the topic or issue at hand.

Further, we find that the way in which we reason and argue can shape that relationship with others. A community of discourse is born when people are willing to enter into relationships in which mutual respect for each other's intelligence and humanity allow them to think, plan, and reach decisions together. It's exciting to launch such a community. However, if you live in a political or social situation in which you would be punished for participating in such a community, you know that it carries a risk to yourself and others. You need to weigh that risk carefully. You might consider your consumer culture to be a sloshing solution from which little critical thinking or ethical practice emerges as precipitate. Your social life or job situation may seem non-intellectual. However, do not be hasty to dismiss it as anti-intellectual. Even the dullest of us need to belong to a discourse community where we can be heard and think together about what matters for us. Stay motivated to be part of a community of discourse because you're meeting a true and abiding human need. Be determined and diligent in finding, making, or stealing a niche for it. You'll be amazed at how people respond.

But communities die too. Suppose you have an argument to share which is necessary for the welfare of the individual members of a community of discourse, but which is likely to cause divisions so deep that the community itself might not survive that argument. Although the principle of conflict helps to a point, it does not guarantee that a certain conflict might not be terminal for the group.

Could members of the community proceed in good faith to risk such an argument even at the cost of losing their community? That's a difficult question. It may be that the community is winding down and coming to an end, which is the very reason that the controversial argument is now emerging. If so, then perhaps newly constituted communities are needed to carry the reasoning further. We aren't so much sacrificing the community for the sake of the argument as we are allowing the community to disband so that new communities might emerge. Even a sturdy and worthwhile community of discourse isn't necessarily, for those reasons, a perpetual institution.

So why invest time and effort in trying to be part of such a community? It's in such company that you learn active listening and thoughtful speaking. Without those skills, you can't show respect for yourself or others. It's in such company that you are more likely to hear different perspectives on an issue. It's in such company that you *feel* more human. How should you feel about yourself and others when you argue in the community of discourse to which you belong? Members should feel:

1. That their intelligence and humanity matters to each other;
2. That they are more motivated to learn more about the issue at hand;
3. That they are more fully human (greater sense of dignity, personal satisfaction, or fellowship with others) for having participated in this discourse than they would feel otherwise;
4. That they do not experience the argument as futile or abusive, even if it was difficult, contested, and did not result in complete agreement, but they do have a deepened understanding as a result; and
5. That they can honestly say that they played a part in creating a community of discourse.

That doesn't mean that such a community is composed exclusively of gentility or warm fuzzies. Even when we leave an argument feeling angry or defeated, the argument may be ultimately sustaining for the community. However, if we leave an argument intellectually ashamed of ourselves or others in the community, then the argument has failed to sustain regardless of its logical merit.

As the practice of critical thinking leads us into ethical terrain, we discover that our ability to think and even our motivation to think depends on the community to which we choose to belong, whether it's a group of friends, a profession, or an online collection of people with the same interests. Sometimes the very best situation is one in which we can actually plant the seeds of such a community when we are generous enough with acquaintances to reason with them in such a way that they are encouraged to respect each other's intelligence and humanity and become eager to help each other to think about something which matters for them. Creating a community of discourse happens when there is a pre-existing need to explore and think about issues crucial to that group of people.

You might think your environment doesn't have much potential for such conversations. Again, take confidence in the knowledge that each of us needs to make sense of the world and to find meaning in it. When that need is honored and met, communities of discourse arise in places you would least expect to find them. Even when people seem too apathetic for participation in such communities, they'll respond if that deep need is honestly acknowledged and effectively sustained. Happily, people learn very quickly when they have good role models. A few of those role models can have considerable influence.

I hope that you belong to many such communities in your life. We know what it's like to belong to communities which spend their time in gossip, complaint, busy-ness, fear, or trivia. The good news is that it takes only one or two members of that group to start sustaining arguments ... and no one wants to feel left out. You may be in a community right now that's ripe for such a retrofit. If you understand the principles of sustaining arguments and the skills they require, you can be one of the starters. Good luck!

Sustaining Scenario: Students decided that our puppy's fate was a subject that mattered. These students mattered enough to each other to keep working together on a proposed campus animal shelter. They succeeded in getting the shelter established by offering the university arguments that mattered. Not only was the puppy adopted, but other homeless cats and dogs around campus bene-

fited too. Once you start critical thinking with others, who knows what ethics you can start practicing.

Share No. 46 Read the following passage by Václaw Havel:

> "**The man who hates does not smile, he merely smirks; he is incapable of making a joke, only of bitter ridicule; he can't be genuinely ironic because he can't be ironic about himself. Only those who can laugh at themselves can laugh authentically ... The hater utterly lacks a sense of belonging, of taste, of shame, of objectivity. He lacks the capacity to doubt and ask questions, the awareness of his own transience and the transience of all things ... the common denominator of all this is clearly a tragic, almost metaphysical lack of a sense of proportion. The hateful person has not grasped the measure of things... .**"—The Oslo Conference on "The Anatomy of Hate" from *The Art of the Impossible*—by Václaw Havel (1990)**

This is the least appealing share you've been offered so far, but it may still deliver dividends. You may want to leave it untouched, but don't throw it away. That's up to you. Pick any minority group you wish and go looking for the absolutely worst Internet hate site you can find about this minority. Don't try this unless you have a thick skin and a strong stomach. You will probably be shocked, offended, and outraged by what you uncover. If Havel is right about hatred excluding any real belonging, how is it that such groups manage to not only exist but to flourish? Plainly, they are discourse communities though you might not have any confidence in their critical thinking or ethical practice. For example, some anti-Semitic groups discourse together to deny that the Holocaust ever happened. What, if anything, distinguishes them from substantial communities of discourse? Using what you've found, write an essay answering this question.

Share No. 47 Collecting a dividend on this share will take at least a month, so give it time. Find or start a genuine community of discourse over the next month. It can be a club, professional association, or a group of friends. It's not just a social group such as a high school reunion, or a group with shared interest such as Frisbees or gardening. Your community may have more than one motive or purpose, of course. But at least one motive and purpose for this group is to convene to think about something that matters to them, not just to chat. Describe your community of discourse, and, with reference to the principles and skills of sustaining arguments set forth in this text, explain how your community has proven itself to be an excellent place for ethical argumentation. What benefits have you derived from this community? What is the hardest thing about keeping it together?

Share No. 48. Is new software a gift of new knowledge or is it a commodity which you must pay someone for? Research the Electronic Frontier Foundation. You can find their website at www.eff.org. Review the philosophy of Richard Matthew Stallman and the Free Software Foundation at http://www.gnu.org/philosophy/. You may not have been aware of these communities of discourse. They share a new 21st century idea of what counts as "free knowledge." Inasmuch as the authors of the U.S. Constitution did not anticipate the Internet, we need to decide whether we should claim digital rights as civil liberties. Find out what members of this virtual community of discourse believe and how much you agree or disagree with their platform and the issues in which they're involved. If you wanted to participate in their discussion, where would you begin? Report on how their campaign / crusade can influence how you use the Internet and what that means ethically for you. Share your five-page essay in person with three people and online with three other people.

Share No. 49 Here's another ethical issue tucked inside critical thinking on the Internet. We use the Internet for research, communication, and development of new ideas. It's a tool for critical thinking but it's even more than that. The Internet is also, at times, the ongoing activity of critical thinking. Discourse communities are no less real for being virtual. Likewise, their ethical practice is no less genuine, blameworthy or praiseworthy just because the participants don't meet each other in person. If you own a newspaper or a television station, you influence critical thinking but you also provide a forum for critical thinking. Is that more or less analogous to creating a web site or owning an internet domain? As you and your online partners navigate between sites and domains, what's your ethical relationship to the domainer? Here's your Share No. 49. Introduce yourself to three people online who happen to reside in your geographic community. (No, this is not about dating.) Form a community of discourse as you did in Share No. 47 and sustain it for a few weeks. Next, arrange to meet in person with these three people a number of times over a two week period and try to continue the community of discourse together without use of the internet. The social dynamics may be different, but are they different in any way that matters to the quality of your critical thinking together? Do new ethical issues emerge or does the very frame of discourse ethics change in a way that matters for the participants? Write this up in a five page pages.

Share No. 50 We can argue until the cows come home, so now we've finally arrived. This is the last share for this book, but you can share your own presents with your community. When we decide what's safe to drink, what's good to drink, and what's affordable, we have joined a consumer community. We might not have thought about testing its boundaries or joining a different beverage community. For example, you might not consider drinking cow's milk unless it's first homogenized, pasteurized, and refrigerated and perhaps fortified with vitamins or rendered skim or fat-free. That's very likely in your beverage consumer community. No one may say that raw milk is dangerous or tastes bad, but you may all believe it. So, go to a local dairy farmer and get some raw milk to drink. Discuss with the farmer whether the milk is as healthy as pasteurized or homogenized milk. Find out as much as you can about whether raw milk is good or bad for your health. Find out whether the farmer drinks raw milk. Then discuss this issue with other people who prefer raw milk. You might not think this is an issue of much substance, but find out the views of people who drink it. If your beverage community refuses to take you seriously, it might be more substantial an issue than you supposed. This is scholarship that requires you to swallow what you think is true. If you did decide to drink more raw milk, what kind of new community would you seek or start? Write this up in a four-page essay.

Notes on Sources

The principle of scholarship heavily emphasizes investigation and overcoming obstacles to knowledge, testing the strength of inferences, and evaluating the merits of an argument. I hope that these Notes on Sources apply this principle with adequate objectivity for the thirty-seven sources I quote and reference in the text.

Introduction: Uncovering the Ethics in Critical Thinking

1. *Science and Poetry* by Mary Midgley (2001). This is Dr. Midgley's sustained philosophical and historical argument against reductionism in Western culture. She champions reconciliation between the sciences and the rest of human knowledge, though don't expect any simple formula to ensure this detente. She is hard on philosophers held most culpable for dualism and reductionism, such as Lucretius and Francis Bacon, but a moral philosopher should be relied upon to be a bit moralistic. Her more recent book appeals to James Lovelock's Gaia theory as one way to combat dualism in our knowledge of nature. See *Homage to Gaia: the life of an independent scientist James Lovelock* The moralist approach in *Science and Poetry* is also wielded to great effect in *Wickedness* where she makes short work of sociobiological and popular attempts to justify human violence and cruelty by appeal to the alleged "aggression" of nature.

2. *Air Apparent—How Meteorology Learned to Map, Predict, and*

Dramatize the Weather by Mark Monmonier (1999). Because I love maps, I was already prepared to welcome a book by a geographer. This is not only a wonderful bit of cultural history about how weather maps became so useful but also how they represent one of the best examples of communicating science to the public on a daily basis. Philosophically and historically, it's shocking to learn that the now-familiar idea of mapping weather had to be created from scratch in the early 19th century. Monmonier keeps the weather map information updated online at http://www.press.uchicago.edu/Misc/Chicago/534227ap.html.

Chapter One: Sustaining Arguments

3. *Evolution's Rainbow: Diversity, Gender, and Sexuality in Nature and People* by Joan Roughgarden (2005). Dr. Roughgarden's work of biological criticism argues that her professional community of discourse (biology) should think critically about the facts of gender and sexuality diversity in nature and not assume that the Darwinian theory of sexual selection is entirely adequate for an evolutionary explanation of this data. You should be fascinated by how she makes a substantial issue of something marginalized or ignored by mainstream science. I am reminded of Piattelli-Palmarini's caution in *Inevitable Illusions* that atypical phenomena are not for that reason irrelevant or inconsequential.

4. *The End of Science* by John Horgan (1997). Horgan does worthwhile if pessimistic journalism by interviewing scientists and philosophers about whether science is running out of cultural, financial, and intellectual steam as it comes up against an unyielding and mysterious universe. As a science writer, he knows the turf, and it's hard to avoid deeper questions about just how long a successful method and institution can keep its charm and power in our lives. Because science is such an influential model for what we demand of critical thinking, read some of

these interviews. It's interesting that he takes this end-game approach to science's attempts to explain mysticism in *Rational Mysticism* (2003).

5. *On Killing: The Psychological Cost of Learning to Kill in War and Society* by Lt. Col. David Grossman (1995). Grossman gives us a mix of psychological theory, military history, and anti-violence crusade in this grim but arresting consideration of how people learn to kill despite our biological revulsion against killing humans. As a veteran, Grossman is keenly aware of the post-traumatic cost of committing such violence. How we think about killing affects our ethical standards for war and our view of human nature. The risk here is that the connections between critical scholarship and moralizing are so tight that it's tempting to politicize hastily about the whys and wherefores of killing (e.g. gun massacres in schoolyards).

6. *The Whole Shebang—A State of the Universe(s) Report* by Timothy Ferris (1997). Prof. Ferris has the enviable knack of explaining scientific theories without over-simplifying them. At least the mathematics is manageable for most intelligent readers. He also appreciates the historical development of Western science. If you are curious about cosmology, this will orient you well to the current conversations about the origin and destiny of the universe. His earlier work, *Coming of Age in the Milky Way*, is a readable history of science.

7. *The Nobel Prize: A History of Genius, Controversy, and Prestige* by Burton Feldman (2000). Feldman provides an interesting account of how the famous prize, named for the inventor of dynamite, has been bestowed and what its future might be. That prize is a popular mirror of the best of human intellect or a map noting highest elevations on the topography of cultural intellect. The peace prize might be a map to the depths of the human heart. This prize inspires or guides scholarship in both critical thinking and ethical practice.

8. *Science: Endless Horizons or Golden Age?* by Bently Glass (1971).

Glass provokes us to ask whether progress is really a never-ending ascent to greater knowledge. Like other cultural enterprises, it might encounter diminishing returns as its methods reach their limits. Even with new methods, what if science finds out everything worth knowing? Then what? See whether you agree with Glass' assessment of science's prospects.

9. *Unriddling Our Times: Reflections on the Gathering Cultural Crisis*, ed. Os Guinness (2004). Os Guinness and his co-authors give us an evangelical Christian perspective on a popular cultural history theme of apocalypse or at least the storm of cultural crisis for America in particular. David Aitkin describes Alexander Solzenitsen as a modern day prophet of truth. Though the work has a clear agenda, there is sufficient scholarship to keep it from being entirely a jeremiad.

Chapter Two: Principles and Skills for Ethical Argumentation

10. *The Nichomachean Ethics* by Aristotle. Aristotle wrote this book, dedicated to his father or his son, both of whom were named Nichomachus. It was written in 350 BCE. You can find many translations of the ancient Greek in print and online. Very few books about ethics have been as influential in Western civilization as this one. At times it sounds like a classroom lecture, because Aristotle was a natural taxonomist, classifying anything he intended to understand, including the virtues. We can thank him for the terms "species" and "genus." Some of the ethics will surprise you—had you ever thought of friendship as supremely important to ethical living and moral development?

11. *The Posterior Analytics* by Aristotle. This work by Aristotle on the logic of science and the foundations of knowledge also deals with the intellectual virtues required for understanding and knowledge of different sorts of things. To be fair, Aristotle

claimed that the curiosity for knowledge was the foundation of philosophy. Ironically, the medieval scholastics who inherited Aristotle's intellectual legacy gained a reputation for not prizing curiosity so much as did Aristotle, the archetypal natural scientist. It's doubly ironic that the modern philosophers and scholars of the 17th century had to distance themselves from Aristotle's logic and science in order to make curiosity acceptable and even admirable—and not just an expression of pride and vanity.

12. *Empty Ocean: Plundering the World's Marine Life* written and illustrated by Richard Ellis (2003). Ellis' careful and caring history of the ocean's fauna, including whales, fisheries, sea tortoises, manatees, and coral, certainly buries any myths we might have about the "deep blue sea" being pristine or untouched by man. To his credit, Ellis does not simply sound an alarm. He informs the reader of what threatened treasures we should be alarmed about.

13. *No Future Without Forgiveness* by Archbishop Desmond Tutu (2000). Desmond Tutu gives a history and defense of the Truth and Reconciliation Commission in South Africa which he chaired and shepherded. There's no better challenge for critical thinking than trying to think about and talk about the unthinkable and the unspeakable. That's a good description of the TRC's series of public hearings about apartheid. On one hand, this is sustained inquiry and scholarship about violence. But the critical thinking required to publicly uncover the truth is a dramatic ethical practice for both the accused and the survivors.

14. *Secrets: On The Ethics of Concealment and Revelation* by Sissela Bok (1983). Prof. Bok did philosophy and ethics a real favor with her earlier book on the dark side of communication, *Lying* (1978). *Secrets* carries that forward. Good scholarship must take lying and secrets seriously, because they are obstacles to investigative research. You also need to consider what lying and secrets do to a community of discourse. Good communities

honor some sort of confidentiality to build trust, and practicing this may result in keeping secrets. Is this compatible with sustaining arguments or respecting people? You don't need to be a philosopher to need more thinking on this topic.

15. *Never At Rest — A Biography of Isaac Newton* by Richard S. Westfall (1980). Westfall's account of Isaac Newton's life will persuade you that Newton's thinking was complex, astonishing, embarrassing, deeply private yet a supreme public monument. One of the most famous communities of discourse and scholarship, the Royal Society, was as much his handiwork as an application of Francis Bacon's ideas about scientific research.

16. *Gorilla Suit* by Bob Paris (1997). Bob Paris' early fame as a gay Mr. Universe is followed by this reflection upon what it means to make a career out of one's physique. Since what he discovered and confirmed about muscular development would influence others, he struggles not just with success, but with being a role model and finding the right communities of discourse. Perfectionism is an issue for critical thinking (particularly when seeking mathematical solutions) and bodybuilding is a prime example of perfectionism's costs and rewards. We don't usually think of athletic accomplishments as a form of scholarship, but the path to such accomplishment could be viewed as a scholarly albeit sweaty endeavor.

17. *Algeny* by Jeremy Rifkin (1983). Mr. Rifkin has an extensive career as a public intellectual and is currently President of the Foundation on Economic Trends. His books usually identify an emerging technological or economic trend which he views as problematic or culturally troubling. Though he sometimes has a manifesto of his own to nail to to door in the name of tradition, common sense, humanism, or simply caution, Algeny is an example of scholarship dedicated to keeping society from skidding down the latest slippery slope. In *Algeny*, he made some controversial claims against the Darwinian theory of evolution and against the promises of biotechnology. There have

been better evaluations of Darwin in the past 20 years, and, in view of what biotechnology has become in the past twenty-five years, his investigative alarms are either prophetic or, from the stakeholders' perspective, alarmist.

18. *An Ordinary Man* by Paul Rusesabagina (2006). This is a humble and stirring autobiography by the man who rescued over a thousand people in the middle of the Rwanda genocide in 1994. We sometimes complain that we can't sustain good thinking on a subject if we are too distracted by circumstances. Rusesabagina reminds us that it's in the middle of the worst circumstances that we most desperately need sustaining arguments: arguments which matter, about things which matter, to people who matter to each other. When neighbors are hacking each other to death with machetes, the need is not just to escape but to come to grips.

19. *Resilience Thinking — Sustaining Ecosystems and People in a Changing World* by Brian Walker and David Salt (2006). Walker and Salt's book is a double bonus. It not only provides a succinct and readable presentation of adaptation theory of systems (human, non-human, and the hybrid socio-ecological systems), but it also describes five case studies of environmental challenges from around the world, ranging from the Florida Everglades, the Caribbean corals, Australia's breadbasket (the Goulburn-Broken Catchment), the Kristianstads Vattenrike of Sweden, to the Northern Highlands Lake District in Wisconsin. For critical thinkers, the most interesting aspect of the adaptation strategies in each case is how new communities of discourse have arisen and flourished to deal with the challenges. Those communities themselves have had to be structurally and functionally diverse enough to remain resilient.

20. *The Little Book of Circle Processes — A New/Old Approach to Peacemaking* by Kay Pranis (2005). Kay Pranis developed her modern adaptation of the ancient tribal peace circle in handling a labor dispute within a Minnesota correctional facility.

That's a pretty stiff test. She has since developed a number of purposes for such confidential circles in which participants take turns speaking as they receive the "talking piece." The circle can be used for simple "checking-in," peacemaking, community building, sentencing (jails and prisons), school discipline, and elsewhere. It has a resilient caring and carrying capacity. Kay Pranis offers a lengthier and more in-depth study of this circle format in *Peacemaking Circles: From Crime to Community* (2003).

Chapter Three: Thinking of Fallacies as Ethical Issues

21. *Beyond Freedom and Dignity* by B.F. Skinner (1973). Although behaviorism no longer holds a dominant position in psychological theory, the commercial and therapeutic applications of operant conditioning are legion. If you think that objectivity requires us to observe and study things (including people) only from the outside and that theories which demand this are more scientific and credible than others, Skinner's behaviorist manifesto will show you the cultural collaterals of this research approach.

22. *Why Terrorism Works* by Alan M. Dershowitz (2002) . It may take a courtroom lawyer to deal rationally if not conclusively with with irrational violence. Dershowitz' book as a good critical thinking challenge, particularly on the politics of the Middle East. His novel, *Just Revenge* (2000) does the same for our thinking about retribution as a sustaining argument in the wake of the Holocaust.

23. *The Color Line* by John Hope Franklin (1993) Few people can claim to have contributed so much and for so long to the scholarship of racism as Prof. Franklin. Whether you agree with his position on a given race issue, you'll benefit by the care and depth of his thinking.

24. *Time and the Art of Living* by Robert Grudin (1982). This is a lovely literary work with empathy and some truly poetic reflections on how human beings handle the flow of time. It's a bit partial to how middle-aged humans do this, but it's insightful all the same. The best compliment I can pay this text is that it's eminently quotable.

25. *Zero — The Biography of a Dangerous Idea* by Charles Seife (2000). Seife's book is not extensive historical scholarship but his mathematics is sound and you'll find that thinking about nothing can actually be sustaining. The "dangerous idea" theme may be a bit overdone, but it's not easy keeping the concept of zero in historical and cultural perspective. We take zero for granted, but finding a niche for it in western thought changed the boundaries of thinking itself.

26. *Enquiries concerning Human Understanding* by David Hume (1748). David Hume wrote this text with the hope of making the ideas set forth in his earlier *A Treatise of Human Nature* (1739–1740) more readable and more widely read. Modern psychology makes his radical principles of association sound almost like comfortable common sense. Hume could be quite opinionated, but was usually too thorough a skeptic to be knowingly dogmatic in his account of cognition.

Chapter Four: The Ethical Practice of Doing the Math

27. *Aftermath — Violence and the Remaking of a Self* by Susan J. Brison (2003). Philosopher Susan Brison undertakes the difficult task of recounting her rape and near-murder and interpreting it for a personal and philosophical understanding of the experience of living with the aftermath of traumatic violence. The example of a "surd" is only one instance in which she seeks ways to convey or do justice to how a survivor of violence rein-

vents, restores, and rebuilds a self shattered by violence. You may wonder how a victim of intense personal violence can think critically and authentically about that violence. Brison grapples with that challenge, personally and philosophically. How we decide to think about violence affects our relationships with those who've suffered trauma. Think for yourself: What sort of scholarship about violence would you consider most credible?

28. *The Golden Ratio: The Story of Phi, the World's Most Astonishing Number* by Mario Livio (2002). Livio's mathematical and historical scholarship are fine-tuned. He is merciless but fair in his evaluation of various versions of the phi cult without dipping too deeply into philosophy of mathematics. If nature and culture were truly as dominated by the golden ratio as some enthusiasts claim, what, if anything, would that mean for how we should treat each other, nature, or the world we build? The marriage of words and numbers is not always as pretty as the golden ratio, but who said that unified understanding would be risk-free?

29. *Innumeracy* by John Allen Paulos (1989). Professor Paulos has given us a number of books about the meaning of math in our culture. Though he teaches mathematics at Temple University in Philadelphia, he is first and foremost a public intellectual on behalf of math literacy. His popular text is packed with examples of public math mistakes and chiefly mistakes in wielding math concepts. You may not be convinced that our common good can be secured by better math education, but it's hard to argue against his position that we need to take moral responsibility for innumeracy and its social consequences.

30. *The Logic of Failure* by Dietrich Dönner (1989) trans. By Rita and Robert Kimber, 1996). Donner uses clever models of situations which call for planning and decision-making, but which are also (subjectively) complex, possess intransparent elements and internal dynamics, and are based on an incorrect or in-

complete understanding of the system. The title of his book sounds like an oxymoron, but it's not. The logic of failure means that it can be understood and handled. Henry Petroski's *Success through Failure: The Paradox of Design* (2006) takes this optimism a step further and argues that, particularly in architecture, success is built on the back of design failures. It redeems this sort of scholarship in ways that any good coach would commend.

31. *Inevitable Illusions* by Massimo Piattelli-Palmarini (2007). The author defends and expounds a research tradition in cognitive psychology which frames general departures from rationality as "cognitive illusions." I am reminded of a work thirty years ago by Gustav Ichheiser, *Appearances and Realities* (1970, Jossey-Bass Publishers, Inc.) in which Ichheiser trod some of the same turf though in social rather than cognitive psychology. The topic of illusions carries the scholarly risk of Kant's *ding an sich.* by naming something which is, by definition, an irreducible phenomenon and resists integration into everything else we know, other than what we know about other illusions. That's enough to make any scholar grouse.

32. *"How to Make Cognitive Illusions Disappear: Beyond Heuristics and Biases"* European Review of Social Psychology 2: 83–115 (1991). This article by Gerd Gigerenzer is cognitive ecology. Daniel Kahneman and Amos Tversky's research has created much interest in and controversy about the reality of cognitive illusions, and Gigerenzer's essay is one example. The question is whether the concept of illusion is accurate and appropriate to describe our thinking about probability, whether that thinking consists of strategies, heuristics, or biases.

33. *A Problem From Hell: America and the Age of Genocide* by Samantha Power (2002). When Dr. Powers visited Bosnia in the early 1990's as a graduate student, she did not intend to become an authority on genocide. Perhaps the issue chose her. She is the first to complain that Americans would much rather talk about

genocide than prevent it, stop it, or punish it. So, public speaking on this subject must be vexing for her. Dr. Powers book argues that when we critically think about the unthinkable (genocide), we can't avoid the ethical mystery of why those with knowledge, opportunity, power, and values to intervene do nothing. Genocide is therefore difficult to think about for more than one reason.

Chapter Five: Finding a Community of Discourse

34. *The Philosophy of Loyalty* by Josiah Royce (1908). Josiah Royce is not much like his pragmatic philosopher friend and rival, William James. His book is based upon a series of lectures which can be viewed as a scholar's response to James' own series of lectures. Royce's loyalty is pledged to German idealism. Consequently, World War I was spiritually as well as politically disillusioning for Royce. He argues well that loyalty deserves a place in ethics, despite its problematic partiality and excesses. Twentieth century history could be described as too much loyalty gone too bad. Still, this virtue has an important role in a community of discourse. There's the loyalty of friendship, loyalty to an idea or cause, and loyalty to shared values, so we have the potential of others pledging these loyalties or else betraying them.

35. *Public Intellectuals—A Study of Decline* by Richard Posner (2001). Judge Posner argues that critical commentary for the common good has deteriorated over the past 70 years. Before we figure out who or what to blame, think of the public intellectual as a member and perhaps founder of a necessary community of discourse. Otherwise, this role truly does devolve into a lone voice crying or carping in the wilderness. Posner's cultural history will give you inspirational as well as cautionary tales about those who have stepped up to this challenge.

36. *The Art of the Impossible: Politics as Morality in Practice* by Václaw Havel (1990). The speeches of playwright and Czech president Havel. He has an artist's eye and a dissident's justified suspicions about the effect of totalitarian systems upon critical thinking and human relationships. *The Ethical Practice of Critical Thinking* doesn't deal with political violence against freedom of association. Scholarship does not occur in a political or social vacuum. The lack of such freedom makes a community of discourse riskier.

37. *The Theory of Communicative Action* by Jürgen Habermas (1981). Habermas' emphasis upon reason as embedded in community is a formal theoretical approach to rationality as communicative or interpersonal reason. His work is most often associated with "communities of discourse." To appreciate Habermas' theory, it's best to be familiar with Immanuel Kant's concept of rationality, and the imperatives required for its existence. *The Ethical Practice of Critical Thinking* does not argue for or against universal standards and rules for communities of discourse, but it does outline some of the ethical principles and skills that appear shared by a wide range of critical thinking communities.

Name Index

Index